SHELDON NORD

Judicious Leadership

for residence hall living

Forrest Gathercoal

Judicious Leadership for Residence Hall Living
By Forrest Gathercoal

Copyright 1991 by Forrest Gathercoal

Published by **Caddo Gap Press**
    915 L Street
    Suite C-414
    Sacramento, California 95814

Price - $9.95

ISBN 0-9625945-9-8
Library of Congress Catalog Card Number 91-073960

CONTENTS

ACKNOWLEDGMENTS

I wish to gratefully acknowledge and express my appreciation to Corday Goddard for the "spark" which led to the development of this book, Elizabeth Elam for her help in nurturing these ideas, and to their Resident Advisors in Wilson Hall and Finley Hall on the campus of Oregon State University--Jeff Albelo, Craig Beals, Danielle Benz, Monica Brante, Maris Dickson, Jon Greenwood, Crystal Hanson, Christopher Joy, Mike Kerbs, John Lawless, Sean McDonald, and Deepak Neopane. A special thanks to Sue Adams, Barbara McEwan, Paulette Ratchford, Richard Romm, and Terri Tower for their enthusiastic support, professional critique, and editorial assistance. An finally to my family, teachers, students, and friends who have shared their lives with me--thanks for being there.

--**Forrest Gathercoal**

PREFACE

As a student years ago I remember one of my elementary teachers who had but one rule in her classroom. Simply stated: "You may do what you want in this classroom until it interferes with the rights of others." It was her way of acknowledging individual differences among students while recognizing the need for an educational environment free from disruptive behavior. By taking this position and applying it in an even-handed manner to student conduct, she was unknowingly teaching and respecting students' constitutional rights. And at the same time, she was creating a classroom environment in which students were able to learn about their responsibilities to the other members of the class.

Judicious Leadership is fashioned upon this principle by creating an ethical and educational perspective for residence hall management cruxed on our nation's *Bill of Rights*. By recognizing college students' citizenship rights, providing them an opportunity to experience individual liberties, and helping them understand the needs and demands of their social responsibilities, we empower residence hall students to govern and

1

think for themselves. Colleges and universities have always believed that teaching citizenship is an important aspect of their educational mission. **Judicious Leadership**, however, takes that belief one step further--for college staff to acknowledge and accept its students as citizens. This democratic environment in residence halls serves as a model for the same system of rules under which students will live when they leave college life.

The book is divided into four parts:

Part I, **Ethics and the Student/Advisor Relationship**, examines responsibility and style, and functions as the conscience of good student management by suggesting ways to create and maintain a professional relationship of trust and care between students and residence hall staff. Successful resolution of problems always flows more easily from a relationship of mutual respect and shared responsibility established by ethical principles of good educational and management practices.

Part II, **A Constitutional Perspective,** is a brief review of the historical background and the law applicable to students in public colleges and universities. It serves as the foundation and provides a framework for developing and carrying out reasonable rules and decisions.

Part III, **Judicious Advising and Management**, introduces and supports an educational management model for student management as opposed to a punishment or confrontive approach in handling student behavior problems. Part III suggests a methodology for helping students learn and experience their individual rights as well as know and appreciate their responsibility for the welfare of others. It also serves as a guide for residence hall staff to develop judicious rules and consequences designed to create and maintain a democratic community in which all students feel they are valued.

Part IV, **Balancing Rights and Responsibilities,** emphasizes the importance of balancing the individual rights and educational needs of one student against the compelling interests of the majority. Offered are strategies and techniques staff will find useful for the implementation of **Judicious Leadership**. In short, it is a wellspring from which residence hall staff can draw as rules and related decisions are formulated accordant with student's special needs and problems. Part IV is not meant to be all inclusive of disciplinary and educational issues facing hall staff, but does provide many examples of incidents and policies which are directly related to student rights and responsibilities in college residence halls.

In summary, **Judicious Leadership** is a leadership style and philosophy based on the synthesis of professional ethics, constitutional law, and good educational management. This book brings together ethical, legal, and proven educational advising principles for the purpose of helping residence hall staff examine all sides of residence hall management issues. Although most staff members will agree that the answers to everyday management problems cannot be quantified into a single publication, a management philosophy can be learned and developed which will reduce the complexities of the sundry daily decisions facing residence hall personnel today.

Judicious Leadership was written for the purpose of empowering residence hall staff to empower their students with the language and know-how needed to establish a campus living environment based on our nation's constitutional principles of freedom, justice, and equality.

PART I

ETHICS AND THE STUDENT/ADVISOR RELATIONSHIP

Ethical practices manifest the conscience of every professional relationship and constitute the acceptable standards of moral and proper conduct. Ethics are sometimes referred to as "beginning where the law stops." For example, there is no law against a residence hall staff member asking a student in the presence of others, "Why don't you grow up and learn to control your drinking?" But the ethics of publicly disclosing students' personal problems is considered poor professional practice, often leading to attitude and behavioral problems. It also has the effect of setting in motion an adversarial relationship which severely limits good communication and any chance of getting to the source of many students' real problems.

The community esteem of every profession, therefore, lies in its ethical practices and conduct. This axiom is no less true for residence hall staff who are responsible for creating and managing a comfortable learning and living environment.

The Student/Advisor Relationship

The ethics of residence hall management are shaped by the advisors' perception of their role in the student/advisor relationship. If residence hall staff believe appropriate social interaction can be learned and practiced in a residence hall setting, and that it is their mission to employ methods and strategies to help students learn and develop attitudes of personal responsibility, then their professional ethics will reflect a **student-centered** approach to hall management. Conversely, staff who view administrative convenience or safeguarding their authority figure status as most important to good management are more **advisor-centered** and therefore would define ethics in disciplinary matters as student behavior which allows them their right to manage.

Or stated another way, advisor-centered staff are usually very busy with "administrivia" and are more likely to believe that their role is not to "babysit" troubled students, but leave them to their own making. While student-centered staff, on the other hand, will view any student contact, whether positive or negative, as an opportunity to play a part in the growth and development of an advisee.

For residence hall staff to become more student-centered in their approach, there must be a style and technique developed to communicate the drama of advising responsibility, an ability to transcend the daily interactions between students and staff. This professional level of communication begins by getting the **Self** out of the way. How does one do this? One rises above self-interests through **enlightenment** and through **effort**. Enlightenment begins by valuing students' personal and academic development over self-interests and desires--thereby creating a style where personal feelings are set aside for the purpose of helping every student succeed. Equally important to enlightenment is acquiring the fundamentals of good management and advising practices. Meetings with other staff, books and articles on communication and advising, seminars and workshops presented on and off campus, as well as just observing others are some of the ways hall staff can build a well-spring of ideas and strategies for creating a good hall environment.

Enlightenment alone, however, is not enough. Developing an effective professional style requires tireless effort and a growth period that eventually leads to a seasoning that comes only from practice, practice, practice. Through enlightenment and effort residence hall staff learn how to equitably manage and care for their students as they lose themselves in the communication process and the activities of the student/advisor relationship. Gradually mechanics are mastered, technique is transcended, and effective student advising and management becomes a natural creativity. By minimizing their own self-consciousness, residence hall staff will begin to experience a feeling of being on top of students' problems and in control of their own self-interests. If an advisor's every thought and act plays off the importance of developing and maintaining the all-important student/advisor relationship, the question to be asked again and again becomes; **how should a responsible residence hall advisor act upon this matter?** When style and technique are sound, students will begin to sense an increased level of trust and confidence which in turn has the effect of empowering hall advisors with feelings of professional competence and responsibility. Residence hall staff will know when they have attained this level of assurance with their students when it becomes natural to respond to troublesome students by saying, "No matter what you call me or how you act, I still really care about you and am going to do everything I can to make living here enjoyable for you and others." In the end, an **Advisor Self** will emerge which then becomes the sustaining force behind an educational and mentoring philosophy funda-

7

mental to a viable student/advisor relationship capable of re-solving even the most difficult of student management problems.

Positive Ethical Practices

Residence hall staff who interact confidently with students and use a "positive role model" approach are more likely to be effective managers than staff who operate from confrontive or defensive positions. To acquire and maintain a positive approach to management is not always easy and often takes study and experience to achieve fully. Whether conscious or subconscious, all professionals believe in some basic, fundamental principles that guide them in their daily activities. From books and articles read, classes and workshops attended, and the day by day interaction with students and colleagues, a professional morality has been shaped in each of us as to how we want to approach our management responsibilities.

Those who take the time to think and talk to their colleagues and students about their professional responsibilities and what principles they value are constantly reminding themselves of the things they should "always" be doing in order to be effective as a residence hall staff member. This type of values clarification with self and others is an excellent way to learn and grow in positions of responsibility. I recommend it highly. As an example of what I mean, I would like to offer the following as guiding principles I have found helpful for me as an educator in providing a focus for my energies and priorities when helping others.

1. **Model responsible professional behavior**. Establishing and maintaining a professional image is important to every profession. Appropriate dress and appearance, good organization, knowledge of what's going on, preparation for meetings, and following through on promises made are only a few

8

examples of modeling behavior congruent with professional responsibility. On the other hand, avoid having loud parties, drinking alcohol in the hall, or having after-hour guests while not allowing students to do the same. Hypocrisy and unbefitting behavior combine to undermine professional integrity and have a negative effect on the efficacy of the student/advisor relationship.

2. **Manifest appropriate personal behavior.** Residence hall staff must avoid expressing inappropriate personal opinions and information about their private lives to students and others within the contextual relationship of their position. For example, whether or not an advisor has ever experimented with drugs or how they feel about some controversial and sensitive social issues, such as abortion, gun control, or religion, should be considered as personal matters and in most cases should be carefully thought through before being disclosed to students. Poor personal hygiene, bigoted expressions, foul language, student harassment, disparaging remarks, and questionable moral conduct are only a few examples of other inappropriate personal behavior uncharacteristic of effective leadership. Residence hall staff serve as role models and risk loss of respect, added behavior problems, and in some cases their positions, as the result of unthinking acts and statements that may unduly influence the more impressionable minds of students under their care.

3. **Develop a judicious style and educational consequences which value students as citizens.** Management by whim and caprice can lead to embarrassment, alienation, and needless behavior problems. When I was a school counselor I would often use analogies to help troubled parents learn to cope with the adolescent behavior of their children. One such analogy was to suggest to parents they begin as soon as possible treating their children as they would a guest in their home. For example, when a guest inadvertently spills food on the floor,

help is usually offered and the guest's apology is quickly accepted. Their children, on the other hand, are usually scolded and forced to clean the mess by themselves, usually to punish as well as to learn responsibility. Not always understood is the fact that a parent's anger followed by a lecture and demeaning remarks is not teaching children prudent table manners or responsibility, but rather to fear mistakes as well as presenting a model of how they someday should treat their own children. A judicious style would treat misbehaving children, as well as students in a residence hall, as citizen-guests and model for them behavior from which they will learn and grow. Staff who seek to understand individual differences among students and thoughtfully balance these differences with the welfare of the majority will enjoy a relationship of mutual respect with their students. Courtesy, dignity, and self-esteem are all-important to a good, strong student/advisor relationship.

4. **Encourage and model an eagerness for helping and advising others**. Just "going through the motions" is usually reflected in student interest and behavior. Enthusiastic staff fired up about the joys and benefits of residence hall living are infectious, often making the difference between students' success in college or contributing to students' misguided decisions to leave. Residence hall staff who are actively listening and learning from their students, developing new ideas and methods of communication, and active in professional activities will continue to experience the rewards of residence hall advising and administration. These staff members seldom tire of their responsibilities and almost never burn out; their flames just continue to burn brighter.

5. **Focus efforts on motivation, encouragement, and building student self-esteem**. Fortunate are the students of residence hall staff who have mastered the art of motivating and encouraging their students. Encouragement depends not so much on concrete actions as on underlying attitudes. The same

10

words spoken to two different students may encourage one and discourage the other. For example, praising one student may lead to increased self-confidence and stimulate further effort, while another may think it was just an accident and not feel motivated toward other positive actions. Therefore, encouragement requires constant observation of the effect. It is more than a single action; it expresses the whole interaction between student and advisor. The tone of voice, the inflection, and incidental inferences may change dramatically the significance of a statement or an action. In short, encouragement is effort and communication that enhances one's intrinsic feeling of self-worth. Students must feel they have value and that their individual needs and desires are considered worthy regardless of their behavior. The ability to encourage and motivate are fundamental tools of good management and the cornerstone of a strong and viable student/advisor relationship.

6. **Accept and appreciate the reality that students behave in a manner they believe is in their best interests at that time.** Students are the best they believe they can be at the time of their behavior--any behavior. Residence hall staff must accept the fact that all previous student behavior was genuine and sincere before they will be able to develop the trust and respect necessary for a student/advisor relationship to be effective.

For example, telling students "I won't help you if you're not going to try to change," is not respecting their previous actions as authentic. It is similar to a lawyer refusing to defend a criminal who refuses to cooperate or a physician removing a patient from a hospital for not taking prescribed medication. Students must be acknowledged and accepted at all times as persons residence hall staff are meant to serve, regardless of their attitudes, behaviors, or the severity of their own problems. A residence hall advisor who "keeps the faith" in each students' ability to succeed in college provides that ray of hope vital to

11

confirming a belief that all are capable of working through problems.

7. **Enjoy residence hall advising and administration and be proud you are in a position to help others**. Perceive behavioral and advising problems as challenges you have accepted and prepared yourself to meet. Hall staff who seek to understand individual differences among their students and thoughtfully balance these differences with the interests of others will enjoy a positive relationship with all members of the living community. Residence hall staff must have confidence that their skills and abilities will make a difference in the attitude and effort of any student they advise, and know in their hearts they are capable, conscientious, and dedicated to helping every student adjust to and enjoy college life.

Disciplinary Practices to Avoid

As countless advising and management problems arise each day, it is often difficult to think of a workable approach or to keep from losing our tempers as we occasionally feel pushed to the wall by a showdown with students. I have learned over the years there is not necessarily a "right" approach or an immediate answer to every problem that comes along. Each situation requires that we look at it from all sides and examine numerous alternatives before making the best decision or taking the most appropriate action. What has proven helpful for me during this process of determining the "best approach" is to keep in mind the management practices that are never successful. I hesitate to think how many times one unthinking remark or icy stare unraveled months of positive interaction and reinforcement. By the expression on a student's face, I knew I should not have done or said what I did. Afterward, too late to recover or help that student, I would vow never to do that again. I eventually discovered that by remembering and avoiding these unsuccessful approaches, I not only kept intact the very important student/educator relationship I had with my students, but I had the time and freedom to be spontaneous and creative in my search for strategies and ideas which eventually proved successful.

With this brief introduction to disciplinary practices to avoid, I would like to respectfully submit my list of "nevers" and recommend that others consider starting their own lists. As with most of life's lessons we learn well, I still wear the scars of mistakes as a reminder that I learned these the hard way--by experiencing them first hand. For this reason, I would like to dedicate the following "nevers" to all my students, past and present, and thank them sincerely for teaching me how an educator should behave.

1. **Never demean a student or group of students.** It always has the effect of diminishing a student's confidence and self-esteem. Sarcasm meant to be clever or a disparaging statement flaunting power or intellect always hurt students, and usually mark the beginning of an adversarial relationship. Most of us learned to accept being put down from well-meaning parents as a way of teaching responsibility or "just keeping the kids in line." I found that in demeaning students, not only did I damage both professional and personal relationships, but, no matter how often or hard I tried, I could never fully regain the student's or group's confidence and respect.

2. **Never summarily dismiss students or send them away**. Ask them if they would like to talk about the problem as a way of getting at the heart of the issue. I always viewed the problem differently after hearing the student's side of the story, which made my next decision a better one than if we had not discussed it. The message you send to all students is a professional one of concern and willingness to help as well as recognize their individual differences.

3. **Never compare students**. People need to feel impor-

tant and know they are valued. Competition often breeds contempt and is simply antithetical to building a feeling of community. Students want to be judged on their own merits and not be thrust by those they want to respect into the shadows of others.

4.   **Never demand respect**; give it to your students. I discovered that by giving it away, it was returned to me many times over. Respect, not unlike love, implies the feelings of another which cannot be taken or demanded. Respect is thoughts and actions one only accords to another.

5.   **Never be dishonest with students**. If I said I would do something, I made every effort to do it. If not, I found an apology was greatly appreciated. Never fear an apology; it is a powerful message to students that they are in the presence of a sincere and honest person. Residence hall staff who are open and authentic will earn the trust and respect needed to hold together an enjoyable and workable student/advisor relationship.

6.   **Never accuse students of not trying** or ask students to try harder; always help them try again or suggest another way. I found accusatory and judgmental statements diminished our relationship and had the opposite effect, making students not want to try at all. Students want learning situations with an encouraging, positive approach, not lectures and negative experiences which alienate and discourage. Accept students' efforts as genuine while communicating a message of faith in their ability to learn other ways. This may appear to be a subtle difference, but students will react with renewed effort and interest.

7.   **Never get into a power struggle**. Sometimes power struggles are difficult to avoid, but with common sense and patience one can become quite good at sidestepping them. If you sense a power play is developing with students, begin by taking your sail out of their wind, and anchor yourself with a long

tether. These are no-win situations and should be handled privately through individual discussions and mutual agreements. Students rarely continue to defy someone considered a friend and one who they feel are on their side.

8. **Never flaunt the fact that you are the one in authority and they are the students.** I would do this during my first year as an educator whenever I felt insecure. I soon realized this decision was made when I was hired and that I did not have to brandish it about at the first sign of conflict. Students usually know when they have messed up and do not need an authority figure preaching to them about it. They need good advice and a friend who will help them recover. If students feel you are sincerely making every effort to help them enjoy and benefit from residence hall living, they will try very hard to help you succeed as a residence hall advisor.

9. **Never become defensive or lose control of your feelings.** When our pride gets in the way, it has a tendency to diminish both our personal and professional qualities. Remarks made during the height of emotional anxiety usually cause frustration and embarrassment for students, and regret on the advisor's part. We should all learn to back off, take a deep breath, and calmly think through a solution that is devoid of emotional overtones. I found that if I did lose control, acknowledged my error, and apologized sincerely, I was considered an up-front educator with human frailties and suffered very little loss of personal or professional respectability.

10. **Never use fear and intimidation to control students.** I would fall back on this approach when I ran out of workable ideas and felt pressured by the situation. I finally recognized that fear and intimidation appeared to work only in the short run, and that its long range effects were unpredictable and often gave rise to other problems. Bitter feelings and sullen attitudes would develop and students became very inventive in the circuitous ways they tried to get back at me for hurting

them. I finally learned ways to back off until I could think of a positive and reasonable approach to the problem.

11. **Never punish the group** for the misbehavior of one of its members. I learned that more often than not the culprit enjoyed the group punishment and the innocent students blamed me for punishing them. Retreat as gracefully as you can if you find yourself in this box, and find another way to handle the situation next time.

12. **Never act too quickly** with a behavioral matter. When I would "shoot from the hip" I invariably said and did things I later regretted. I found that by coming around the problem and avoiding the direct hit approach, errors could be easily corrected and the possibility of both of us saving face was frequently the factor that turned the corner. Unless you have had good results in the past or you are certain that what you are doing is going to work, patience and time can be a great ally.

13. **Never say "you will thank me someday"** as a rationale for something that is perceived by students as not to make sense or have any immediate purpose. I learned that attempting to justify what I was doing by lecturing about future benefits, had little effect on motivating and encouraging students. If learning acceptable behavior had meaning here and now, I did not have to use threats of future difficulties. Make residence hall living inviting to all students with an interesting and challenging management style designed to meet everyone's learning and personality needs. Residence hall staff should want to be "thanked" after each day, as well as "someday" in the future.

14. **Never think being consistent means treating all students alike**. I was always told that one of the characteristics of a good management style is being consistent. It took a few years and numerous bad decisions before I stumbled upon what consistency means to good educators. Consistency in educational management, I have concluded, is being able to identify

individual differences among students day after day, and provide the professional specialization and skills needed to help all students achieve success. Students realize they have different needs and goals and regard highly the staff member who understands that the same method of management and discipline should not be applied to every student. Take the time required to know your students and learn to appreciate and judiciously manage their individual differences.

In Summary

In summary, the ethics of any profession are at best fragile and difficult to manage when put into practice. Because morality is a matter of character, residence hall staff must begin with a general concern for ethical behavior. As the doors to rooms and offices close behind residence hall staff managing their floors and buildings, who is to know if responsible professional ethics will be used to guide all staff actions and decisions? For ethics to be viable, there must be a continuing, on-going moral and ethical inquiry. When residence hall personnel wear well the mantle of their profession, individual biases and personalities take a secondary status to the problems and people they serve. To our students we appear larger than life and, therefore, must personify a model of professional demeanor. It is imperative that we develop and keep alive a strong and viable student/ advisor relationship. In its final analysis, a college residence hall is the student's world.

PART II

A CONSTITUTIONAL PERSPECTIVE

How often do you hear college administrators express their concern and frustration over the plethora of legal issues they are required to understand and implement in colleges today? This feeling of futility is often attributed to a national shift from the parental protectiveness of *in loco parentis*, a legal phrase meaning the college stands in the place of the parent, to the realization that public college students today do have constitutional rights on their campus and in their living organizations. It may be frustrating and time-consuming for many of us to make the change from a parental approach of managing students to a more judicious approach that honors students' civil liberties and respects them as citizens. Now that college students are legally "persons" within the meaning of our constitution, it is essential that residence hall staff in public education today learn both the language of our nation's laws and understand how they apply to the college residence hall setting. In other words, residence halls at public colleges today are in actuality microcosms of the United States of America.

This point is brought home when students confront college

19

administrators with a statement such as, "You can't do that to me, I've got my rights." Asked to explain what they mean by their rights, most respond by saying something like, "I don't know, but all I know is, I've got my rights." Although many students like to use the phrase, few really understand its actual meaning.

The purpose of Part II is to help educators learn to speak and act with self-assurance on the subject of student rights. It provides a brief review of the historical background and the constitutional law applicable to public education. The Constitutional Perspective, therefore, functions as the legal basis of a judicious model for residence hall living.

The Democratic System

Students will move from their residence hall into a system of constitutional government which not only provides for the needs, interests, and welfare of the majority, but bestows specific freedoms on each individual. Individual rights are not guaranteed, but neither are they easily denied by the majority. Growing up in America, most of us learned that democracy is a system of government in which the majority rules. We used this to settle playground arguments by voting on what game to play or seeking a consensus on the rules. Listening to students today, we realize this has not changed. Students continue to learn the concept of "the majority rules," but seldom in their educational or living environment do they learn what it means or have an opportunity to experience the freedoms and responsibilities of individual rights. If college life is the last of their formal education, then it only follows that this may be the last chance for students to learn that in our constitutional democracy individual rights are equally as important as the needs and interests of the majority.

The Bill of Rights

American constitutional liberties spring from the first ten amendments, better known as the *Bill of Rights*. The *First Amendment's* use of the term "freedom" in the context of religion, speech, press, and assembly is generally considered to be one of the most important amendments to the *Constitution*. The clauses "due process of law" and "equal protection" in the *Fourteenth Amendment* are also significant and subject to widespread use and application in civil rights issues. Constitutional clauses are not self explanatory. Their meaning is translated into political, legal, and educational reality largely by the Supreme Court of the United States.

Constitutional rights exist to protect three basic values: freedom, justice, and equality. To live in a free society, however, does not mean we have license to do as we please. The controversy over the question of how, when, and where to limit individual **freedoms** is a never-ending question our society constantly seeks to balance.

The difficulty lies in devising a precise formula to indicate when freedom has exceeded rightful bounds. **Justice** is concerned with due process and deals with basic governmental fairness. Many not familiar with how our laws work sometimes question our justice system when they read or hear about a criminal being set free or an innocent person sent to prison.

An analogy, however, can be drawn between the effectiveness of our nation's justice system with that of our educational system or, for that matter, our nation's medical practices. Although one is designed to help students learn and the other to heal the sick and injured, as with our legal system, neither is entirely successful.

Many agree these systems may be well-conceived and that sincere effort is being put forth, but because of the "human factor," these systems occasionally fail and simply are not equal to the task in every case.

Finally, **equality** presents us with the problem of distributing burdens and benefits. The proposition that "all people are created equal" has never meant that we all possess the same abilities, interests, or talents. These three values--freedom, justice and equality--have their antecedents in the United States *Constitution* and are basic to understanding student's civil rights.

Student Rights

Students who say, "I've got my rights," are for the most part referring to the *First, Fourth,* and *Fourteenthth Amendments.* Although other amendments and legislative laws are occasionally applied to college student learning and behavior issues, residence hall staff knowledgeable about these three amendments have a solid foundation when talking about student rights.

The First Amendment
Congress shall make no law respecting an establishment of religion or prohibiting the free exercise thereof; or abridging the freedom of speech or of the press; or of the people peaceably to assemble, and to petition the government for a redress of grievances.

The *First Amendment* was designed to insure certain basic personal freedoms, which until the 1960s, were seldom applied to students in American public colleges. However, in recent years, numerous judicial decisions related to matters concerning free speech have been litigated. Freedom of the press has also generated considerable litigation concerning student rights

22

to publish and distribute material on college premises. Further-more, the free exercise and establishment clauses in the *First Amendment* which relate to religion continue to have an impact on public educational programs. The right of students to as-semble peaceably has been controversial on American cam-puses for some time, especially during the Civil Rights and Peace Movement years.

The Fourth Amendment
The right of the people to be secure in their persons, houses, papers, and effects, against unreasonable searches and seizures, shall not be violated, and no warrants shall issue, but upon probable cause, supported by oath or affirmation, and particularly describing the place to be searched, and the persons or things to be seized.

This amendment presents an issue of practical importance to all residence hall staff. A student's expectancy of privacy can range from the posting of names for disciplinary reasons to a strip search for suspected concealment of drugs. Most staff members do not consider themselves to have the same societal charge as that of law enforcement officers. However, effective hall discipline and management require residence hall staff to use similar guidelines when taking property from students.

The Fourteenth Amendment
All persons born or naturalized in the United States, and subject to the jurisdiction thereof, are citizens of the United States and of the State wherein they reside. No State shall make or enforce any law which shall abridge the privi-leges or immunities of citizens of the United

> *States; nor shall any State deprive any person of life, liberty, or property, without due process of law; nor deny to any person within its jurisdiction the equal protection of the laws.*

The last two clauses of the *Fourteenth Amendment* have had significant impact on public education. The first of these, known as the **"due process"** clause, provides the legal basis for reasonable rules and a fair and open process for denying student rights. The last clause, known as the **"equal protection"** clause, serves as the constitutional foundation for all our laws and rules prohibiting discrimination. This clause is broadly interpreted in cases dealing with all forms of discrimination including sex, race, national origin, handicaps, marital status, age, and religion, and assures an equal educational opportunity for all students.

In short, the *Fourteenth Amendment* acts as the fulcrum; allowing our somewhat fragile constitutional form of government to balance the welfare of the majority with the countless needs and desires of individuals in our culturally rich and diverse society. Residence hall staff who understand, and are able to apply the concepts of due process, are usually perceived as possessing a sense of fairness and compassion when working with student problems. Because of its importance, the next several pages have been devoted to expanding on the meaning of due process.

Due Process

> *....nor shall any State deprive any person of life, liberty or property, without due process of law;....*

Picture the blindfolded woman symbolizing justice standing strong and confident, adorning the thresholds of our country's

24

courthouses, her outstretched arm holding the familiar scales of justice. Imagine one scale heaped to the brim with all the students in your residence hall actively engaged in their studies and activities. On the other side of the scale, picture one lone student standing with luggage and lap top computer in hand, gazing apprehensively at all of the students amassed on the other side. This graphic illustration symbolizes balancing the interests of one student with those of the majority and is the essence of "due process" as applied to public college residence hall living.

In its simplest terms, due process is a legal effort to balance individual rights with the need to protect the welfare and interests of society. Only when the state is able to show a compelling reason why public welfare should weigh more than individual rights, will the court's scale of justice swing toward the interests of the majority. Conversely, if the government cannot demonstrate a **compelling state interest**, then the rights of a single student will weigh more heavily than all who crowd the other side of the scale. As the scales of justice tip in favor of the minority, judicious leadership would make every effort to help the majority learn tolerance, respect, and consideration for the feelings and individual human rights of others.

Although written succinctly, the Due Process Clause represents two hundred years of legislation and court decisions clarifying and interpreting its meaning. To fully understand and appreciate the complexity of this constitutional concept, it is important we take time to examine the clause a few words at a time.

"**...nor shall any State**" means that in order to have a right to due process there must be state action. When applied to education, only students and faculty in **public** colleges and universities enjoy due process rights; their counterparts in our nation's private institutions do not enjoy due process rights. The legal rights of students and faculty in the private sector are expressly set out in the contract between students and the corporation which administers the school. Speaking in legal terms, students who are dismissed from private colleges would therefore be considered guilty of breaching their part of the contract between them and the institution. The logic of the law implies that students who disobey or are not satisfied with the rules of a private college are admittedly free to choose another. Conversely, public funding of state institutions creates the state action necessary for students' rights to due process in public colleges and universities.

"...**deprive any person**" means withholding these due process rights from anyone who is not legally a person within the meaning of the *Constitution*. For example, the law includes non-citizens as well as those who are in the United States illegally. This is not to say that illegal aliens have a right to live here, but they do have the right to due process while living here, including the right to legal proceedings which may lead to their deportation. "Any person" is broadly interpreted by the courts and today includes all students in our public colleges and universities.

"...**of life, liberty, or property**" defines those rights which may be deprived through due process by governmental action. It is interesting to note that the framers of our *Constitution* used just three words to protect our past, present, future, and even death at the hands of the government. For example, the word "property" includes everything a person legally owns and has acquired up to the present. It covers such tangible properties as real estate, personal property, and money, as well as intangibles like contracts of employment, eligibility and entitlement to welfare payments, and the civil rights of students who attend public colleges and universities.

The second word, "**liberty**," begins with the present and embodies all future acquisitions and aspirations:

...it denotes not merely freedom from bodily

restraint but also the right of the individual to contract, to engage in any of the common occupations of life, to acquire useful knowledge, to marry, establish a home and bring up children, to worship God according to the dictates of his own conscience, and generally to enjoy those privileges long recognized...as essential to the orderly pursuit of happiness by free men. (*Meyer v. Nebraska* 262 US 390, 399 [1923].)

Too often the liberty issue is overlooked for the more understood and simpler applied property aspect. Residence hall staff devoted to helping students succeed, and who sincerely care about their future opportunities, exemplify the importance of liberty within the meaning and spirit of constitutional rights and as a result, often enjoy a special place as a role model and mentor to their students.

Finally, the word **"life"** refers to the loss of personal life at the hands of the government, such as the execution of a criminal. Stated in positive terms, the government may deprive a person of life, liberty, or property only after an individual has been provided due process.

"...**without due process of law**" means the process which is due persons by the local, state, and federal governments. Clarifying its application to everyday situations, court decisions have separated "due process" into two distinct aspects: **substantive** and **procedural**.

"Substantive" due process pertains to the legislation, the rule, or the law itself, and means a basic fairness in the substance of the decision. If the state attempted to deprive a person of life, liberty, or property, substantive due process would require a valid objective and means that are reasonably calculated to achieve the objective. The rule should:

1. Have some rational need for its adoption;
2. Be as good in meeting the need as any alter-

native that reasonable people would have developed;
3. Be supported by relevant and substantial evidence and findings of fact.
In other words, substantive due process implies that laws and decisions must be legal before our government can legally deprive someone of their life, liberty, or property. Whenever someone questions or seeks clarification of a rule or decision, that individual would be legally exercising their *Fourteenth Amendment* substantive due process rights.

"**Procedural**" **due process** relates to the decision-making process used when determining whether a rule or law has been violated. Basic fairness in adjudication is required and has been interpreted by the courts to include the following:
1. Adequate notice.
2. A fair and impartial hearing.
3. The right to appeal the decision.

Adequate notice includes such procedures as charges, evidence to be used against the person charged, a reasonable amount of time to prepare a defense, the time and place of the hearing, and adequacy of form (oral and written). **A fair and impartial hearing** encompasses elements such as a meaningful opportunity to be heard, state a position, and present witnesses. It also may include the right to counsel, presentation and cross-examination of witnesses, and review written reports in advance of the hearing. **The right of appeal** is not only applicable to our state and federal court system, but is an integral part of our governmental structure as students exhaust their administrative remedies by appealing rules and decisions made by residence hall staff.

With few exceptions, the Due Process Clause allows all administrative interpretations and decisions, as well as the rule in question, to be appealed through an institution's administrative structure. From the institution, the decision or rule may be appealed to a higher state or federal administrative agency and then referred to an appropriate court. Every rule or decision made in a public institution is subject to review by another person, board, or court. An administrator who says, "This is a non-appealable decision," is bluffing. Many are unaware students have this right of appeal and that it is possible for their decision or rule to someday reach the United States Supreme Court. Due process, as is the case with many legal concepts, resists a simple dictionary definition and tends to be a dynamic rather than a static concept.

Other Amendments

Although the *First, Fourth,* and *Fourteenth Amendments* are most often cited, some familiarity with the *Fifth, Eighth, Ninth,* and *Tenth Amendments* could be helpful. The self-incrimination clause of the ***Fifth Amendment*** is only applicable in questions of criminal activity and therefore not relevant in residence hall matters between students and staff where the legal relationship is civil law. The ***Eighth Amendment*** prohibits excessive bail and fines and protects citizens from cruel and unusual punishment. While this amendment has appeared often in suits challenging the treatment of prisoners or other persons involuntarily institutionalized, it has not been applied to situations involving students in colleges and universities.

The ***Ninth Amendment*** stipulates that the rights enumerated in the United States *Constitution* shall not be construed to deny or disparage other rights retained by the people. This amendment supports other freedom arguments and has appeared in educational litigation dealing with the assertion of rights to personal privacy by students. It has also been successfully interwoven with other amendments that provide for our basic personal freedoms.

The ***Tenth Amendment***, often referred to as the reserved-powers clause, states; "The powers not delegated to the United

States by the *Constitution*, nor prohibited by it to the States, are reserved to the States respectively, of the people." The United States *Constitution* does not provide a legal base for public education in America. Hence, this amendment has been the underpinning for any state assuming the primary responsibility for public colleges and universities. Our Federal *Constitution*, however, is the source of all of our nation's laws and generally supercedes state law wherever there is a direct conflict between Federal and State governments.

A Pocket-Sized History of College Rules and Practices

Until 1961, court decisions historically supported the concept of *in loco parentis*, which granted to colleges the same legal authority over students as that of a parent. In the absence of "state action," implicit in the *Fourteenth Amendment*, children who live with parents or legal guardians enjoy no constitutional rights. For example, parents searching their daughter's bedroom without a search warrant would not violate her *Fourth Amendment* rights from unreasonable search or seizure, or a son denied use of the family car for the evening would have no Due Process rights to appeal his parent's decision.

The legal concept of *in loco parentis*, therefore, allowed colleges the same ultimate authority as a student's parent. The only exceptions were college rules and decisions which were found by courts to be unreasonable, capricious, arbitrary, malicious, or made in bad faith. The courts generally agreed that college and university authorities were more knowledgeable about matters of student development and discipline than were judges and juries.

Today the law is much different. Courts rarely use the concept of *in loco parentis* when writing opinions on student issues. This legal concept has been replaced by language which addresses the constitutional rights and responsibilities of col-

30

lege students. The *Dixon v. Alabama State Board of Education*
(294 F.2nd 150) case in 1961 was the first significant United
States court decision in which students successfully challenged
institutional authority. This landmark case involved the arbitrary and summary dismissal of students who participated in an
off-campus lunch counter "sit-in" and other civil rights activities which allegedly disrupted campus life. The students were
not given any notice or hearing and were advised of their
dismissals by letter. The issue was whether *Fourteenth Amendment* "due process" required notice and an opportunity to be
heard before students at a tax-supported college could be
dismissed for misconduct. The court stated in part:

> ....It must be conceded, as was held by the
> district court, that power [of the government] is
> not unlimited and cannot be arbitrarily exer-
> cised. Admittedly, there must be some reason-
> able and constitutional ground for expulsion or
> the courts would have a duty to require rein-
> statement. The possibility of arbitrary action is
> not excluded by the existence of reasonable
> regulations.

Eight years later, in 1969, the United States Supreme Court
in *Tinker v. Des Moines Independent School District* (393 U.S.
503) for the first time held that students in public elementary
and secondary schools have constitutional rights in the area of
student discipline. The case, cited ritualistically by school
authorities as well as student plaintiffs, establishes general
guidelines applicable to many school situations. This case
involved high school students suspended by their principal for
wearing black arm bands to school protesting the United States'
involvement in Vietnam. The students won the right to express
their political beliefs when the court stated for the first time:

> ...First Amendment rights, applied in light of
> the special characteristics of the school environ-

31

ment, are available to teachers and students. It can hardly be argued that either students or teachers shed their constitutional rights to freedom of speech or expression at the schoolhouse gate...

It is apparent that times have changed from the days when college and university rules resembled those used in most families. Today, the rules college authorities use must recognize and take into consideration the constitutional rights of students. If, in fact, students do not shed their constitutional rights at the gate, a graphic illustration of the students' rights might be to imagine college students dressing each morning in attire selected from their wardrobe of liberties. By the time they have donned their mail of "freedom," buckled on a sword of "justice," and grasped the shield of "equality," they might be reminiscent of knights of King Arthur's Round Table in full battle dress, as they walk the hallways of our residence halls. This could be seen as a formidable image and possibly intimidating to many residence hall staff who come face to face with student rights issues every day.

To complicate matters even more, college administrators frustrated by the thought of student rights often think to themselves, "The students seem to have more rights than I have." This, in fact, happens to be true. Residence hall staff have no constitutional rights in the student/advisor relationship. Staff has the legal responsibility of respecting and ensuring student rights, but they do not enjoy the same rights from their students.

The constitutional rights residence hall staff do have are those which flow between them and the college. In other words, staff rights come down to them from the employer/employee relationship, not up to them from the student/advisor relationship. Residence hall staff should begin thinking in terms of the students as having the "rights" and of themselves as having the legal and professional "responsibilities" to ensure those rights and the welfare of their students.

We are now at the core, the very heart and soul of the question facing residence hall staff today. **Is there a way to establish and maintain an effective living and learning environment in our residence halls, while at the same time respecting student rights of freedom, justice, and equality?**

The answer, of course, is **yes**, and it all has to do with the **judicious balancing of rights and welfare.** As foreboding as recognizing and respecting student's constitutional rights appear at first blush, there is another very important side to the scale of justice. There are, in fact, four sagacious and time-tested public interest arguments crafted in the courts and construed for the precise purpose of limiting constitutionally protected freedoms. These arguments are as genuine and well-grounded in legal principle and history as the line of reasoning which allows for individual rights.

This legal concept is commonly referred to as a **"compelling state interest"** and simply means that in some conflicts between an individual and society the welfare and interests of the majority will weigh greater than those of the individual--any individual. One of the distinguishing characteristics of **Judicious Leadership** is that it helps students understand and appreciate society's desideratum and its applicability to public college and university environs.

Compelling State Interest

Prior to the 1960s, when a hall staff member was asked by a student to explain the reason for a rule, the response could have been something like: "Because I am your hall director and this is the way we do it here," or "You will have to learn to follow rules someday so you might as well learn to follow mine." The response was usually arbitrary and known as rules for rules' sake--much like a parent's response to the same question at home. A student today, however, questioning the reason for a rule, should hear a response such as: "Let me tell you our college's compelling state interest for the rule." Although the rule may be the same in both situations, today the language and administrative posture has changed substantially in order to respect students' right to know and question the reasons for rules and decisions.

The legality of a college rule is generally presumed, and the burden of proof rests on the complaining student. However, if a rule actually infringes on a fundamental constitutional right, the burden of proof then shifts to school officials to demonstrate a compelling state need. The closer laws come to encroaching on students' substantive rights, the greater the need for justification and clarification by school authorities.

Therefore, a rule which deprives a student of substantive or procedural due process rights must be directly related to the welfare of the college living organization. For example, the need to maintain a proper living and learning environment is a compelling state interest which allows residence halls to legally prohibit excessive noise during study hours or other similar conduct detrimental to these ends.

Now that it is clear college administrators must have a compelling state interest to sustain their rules and decisions, this begs the question: **What are these compelling state interests?** For years our nation's courts have been using four basic arguments in an effort to sustain the balance between the individual and the state's interest in our public colleges and universities.

These compelling state interests are:
1. Property loss or damage.
2. Legitimate educational purpose.
3. Health and safety.

4. Serious disruption of the educational living environment.

Residence hall rules and decisions based on these four arguments will, in all probability, withstand the test of today's court rulings despite the fact that they may deny students their individual rights. Residence hall staff not only have a legal right to deny student constitutional rights, but it is their professional responsibility to prohibit student behaviors when the exercise of those rights seriously affects the welfare of the college.

This governmental control of student rights is generally accomplished by controlling the reasonable **time, place, and manner** of student activities. For example, staff cannot ban from residence halls student expression about controversial political issues, but they can insist on a reasonable time, place, and manner of its dissemination. As officers of the state, it is clearly residence hall staffs' duty to maintain a safe and proper living and educational environment.

Property Loss and Damage

* *"Lounge furniture should remain in the lounge."*
* *"Respect the property of others."*
* *"Return the athletic equipment when you are finished."*

Care and protection of property is usually easy for students to accept and few argue their right to damage school facilities or take the property of others. However, during their college years students have many opportunities to remove or perhaps damage state-owned property as well as personal belongings of others. Taxpayers, therefore, rely heavily on the sound judgment of residence hall staff to oversee the care and maintenance of public property entrusted to them.

Further, students also depend on school personnel to assist in protecting their property while within the jurisdiction of college authority. Rules protecting property should be explicit, fair, and reasonably related to the loss or damage intended to be prevented in order to insure adequate notice and proper protection.

Legitimate Educational Purpose
* *"Freshmen within one year of high school graduation must live in college sponsored housing."*
* *"Quiet hours begin at 7 p.m.."*
* *"Required study table Sunday through Thursday."*

The public mandates college and university administrators manage living organizations consistent with state and federal law. They are considered the experts in matters of academic achievement as well as acceptable campus behavior. Courts are reluctant to second-guess educational or behavioral decisions which are based on sound professional judgment. Generally speaking, all policies and decisions having a tenable educational motive related to appropriate group living objectives come within the intent of this standard.

Requiring younger students to live in residences halls is a good example of the college's authority to regulate behavior which contributes to students' adjustment to student life. Students living on campus would benefit educationally from the experience in self-government, community living, and group discipline, and the opportunities for relationships with staff members. In addition, they have easy access to study facilities and to films and discussion groups.

As students obtain jobs or deal with governmental agencies, legitimate educational purpose changes and becomes legitimate employer purpose or, if dealing with law enforcement, it becomes legitimate police purpose. This would be a reasonable analogy to use when students question what may appear to be arbitrary rules and decisions based on this compelling state interest.

Threat to Health and Safety
* *"Horseplay, skateboarding, etc. outside the building."*
* *"Fire escape doors must be closed by 11 PM."*
* *"Students must have proof of vaccinations before registering for college."*

A fundamental purpose of government is to protect the health (physical, mental, and emotional) and welfare of its citizens and, especially, students who assume they are in the protective environment of the public college they attend. Courts consistently sustain rules and decisions designed to maintain the health and safety of the majority, and are quick to deny individual freedoms in such matters.

The importance of health and safety rules is apparent in residence hall situations which expose students to the dangers of assaults from outsiders, improperly maintained premises, and poor supervision, as well as matters relating to student's emotional and physical health. Although students may complain about rules which prohibit rough play and pervasively vulgar language, or that require periodic inspections, college authorities must take steps to deny jeopardous student behavior in order to ensure the health and safety of themselves and others. If student rights are on a collision course with the likelihood of an injury, the decision must be to protect the interests of the majority. Rules concerned with students' health and safety must be all inclusive, conspicuous, and rigorously enforced.

Serious Disruption
of the Educational Living Environment
* *"Keep the noise level down in your rooms."*

37

> * *"Room parties should remain small and quiet."*
> * *"Avoid the use of `fighting words' and harass-*
> *ing behavior."*

The establishment and enforcement of rules that foster and encourage a proper campus living environment are necessary to the efficient and successful operation of every residence hall. School officials have both the legal authority and the professional responsibility to deny student rights which seriously disrupt student living and learning. Each situation must be decided on its own merits and may vary from one floor to another in the same building.

For example, the usual shouts and laughter of a floor celebrating an intramural win would not necessarily be a serious disruption whereas the same hubbub on another floor which does not involve the general interest of its students would be an unnecessary disruption.

Students must understand that their rights do not allow them to do as they please. Rights are quickly denied when individual actions infringe on the property and well-being of others, or become a serious disruption of the educational living environment. On the other hand, there is a professional responsibility on the part of residence hall staff to carefully weigh student human rights as they bring about the educational and living equanimity envisioned by America's public.

The best way to balance these rights is to help students think and act in a reasonable time, place, and manner as they learn how to legally exercise their rights. This is not easily accomplished. Balancing the obligation to provide for the liberties of a single student with the pressures brought about by the clamor of the majority can add up to a lot of heat in the residence hall kitchen.

Because of the thin line college and university administrators must tread, there may well be a need to view rules and decisions from a constitutional perspective in order to provide a well-regulated and orderly climate for residence hall living.

PART III

JUDICIOUS ADVISING
AND MANAGEMENT

One of the more glaring contradictions in college living organizations today is the autocratic approach many residence halls use to prepare their students to be responsible citizens in a democratic society. Students live under a management system of rules and decisions not unlike the authority they encountered at home, an authority which rewards obedience, punishes offenders, and needs no justification other than "I am the authority here." It is no surprise then that hall staff are continually asking their students, "When are you going to grow up and begin thinking for yourself?"

When hall management parallels this parenting type of autocratic environment, it only follows that residence hall staff may be just another contributing factor in preparing graduates who are less likely to understand or function well in a participatory society. Many who have tried have found that in the long run the benefits of enabling students to think and act as responsible citizens far outweigh the disciplinary expediency of arbitrary rules, confrontive enforcement practices, and predetermined consequences.

Part III develops a framework for rules and consequences designed to alleviate this dichotomy between residence halls and the greater American community. This part integrates our nation's legal principles with an educational model for teaching students about their individual rights and freedoms along with their responsibility for the welfare of others. As a result, residence hall students will not only be regarded and respected as citizens and learn to be responsible for themselves in a democratic living organization, but will have an opportunity to experience the joys and sorrows of being accountable for their own actions.

An Advising and Educational Model

College residence hall advisors must begin by fighting the tendency to "parent" students; as an alternative, they should respect them as citizens capable of living in a democratic community. Too often residence hall staff find themselves inventing an endless parade of rules, hoping to create the illusion of being in control. Many are convinced that confronting students with "a line in the dirt," and the fear of punishment for crossing it, is the way to force responsibility and maintain effective hall discipline.

One problem with this approach is that once students no longer fear the punishment, the "line" is crossed, and the illusion of control begins to unravel, becoming volatile at best. Until students' individual interests are respected and they begin to feel a proprietary interest in their living organization, control of a good learning environment will always be at risk.

Residence hall personnel must learn to move away from the appearance of a staff-imposed "hard-line" method, to a democratic and educational approach emphasizing their skills and abilities as educational leaders. Students are far more likely to develop a conscientious attitude and become accountable to

42

others in the hall when they are provided an opportunity to study and actively participate in a democratic learning environment. When they waver from judiciously imposed boundaries, they need professional hall staff nearby, not a parent substitute or a quasi law enforcement officer to pull them back into line. When a behavior problem does occur it is an unswerving and dedicated staff member who pauses to think--"What needs to be learned here?". Every student problem then becomes an educational and advising challenge.

How much more effective our residence halls could be if we would teach the rationale for society's boundaries and the values of tolerance, understanding, and the need for open-minded communication. Residence hall staff must learn to approach management as educators and advisors finding ways to help students learn and develop attitudes necessary to live responsibly in a campus community.

Judicious Leadership Vs. Confrontation and Punishment

Many college administrators believe a system of confronting students with the rules and the threat of punishment is the best approach to residence hall discipline. They feel once the rules and consequences are established, their responsibility is to be consistent as they play out a predetermined and declared plan of action. Furthermore, they are convinced that to bend the rules or treat some students differently would not be fair to the others. The argument is often made that students know what the rules are and should not be surprised or even upset over paying the consequences for their wrongdoing.

This line of reasoning leads to the conclusion that punitive actions are what students will experience in the "real world" and that punishment, or the fear of punishment, will in the long run teach them to be responsible citizens.

This rules-and-punishment approach to residence hall management feeds upon the appearance of justice and seems to have immediate results with most students. Upon closer scrutiny, however, this approach may actually be antithetical to the college's educational mission, the professional objectives of residence hall staff, and more often than not make worse an already difficult situation.

Many students who feel punished, regardless of the staff member's intent, imitate that same condemning behavior and believe they have license to reciprocate, by either thinking it or actually doing something to punish the staff member in return. This retaliatory urge sets in motion a negative attitude which stifles constructive participation, dampens enthusiasm for residence hall living, and begins to drive a wedge between students and hall staff. This failure of the all-important student/advisor relationship leads almost immediately to an escalation of behavior problems. An adversarial relationship now begins to develop between the staff and students. If the consequences are too severe, students may learn to lie, cheat, withdraw, or end up dropping out of school. When students feel estranged in the student/advisor relationship, they lose an advisor and friend and often turn to others less able to help them work through problems.

Too often residence hall personnel are more concerned with correcting deficiencies than developing and using strategies to change student attitudes. What do we need to do then to change student attitudes? The student/advisor relationship provides an excellent vehicle for helping students change as it brings into play the expertise and resources of many well-qualified communicators, counselors, advisors, mentors, role models, and personnel with patience, knowledge, understanding, empathy, and an unyielding commitment to helping students. These resources should be directed in positive ways toward changing students' attitudes and helping them learn to live within the college's expectations. The measure of student success in all likelihood will be directly related to the quality of trust and mutual respect in the student/advisor relationship and the establishment of a sense of community among the students and their residence hall staff.

If a judicious model is going to work, residence hall staff must have patience as well as skill and knowledge about how to communicate effectively with their students. And if staff are offended by certain student attitudes, such as belligerence, vulgarity, or certain moral values, they must begin by changing their way of thinking before they can successfully deal with those students. A discouraged or intolerant advisor can seldom, if ever, communicate the compassion, resolve, and understanding needed to help students work out their problems. Staff who have the ability and resourcefulness to help change student attitudes and clarify their goals are long remembered and play a significant role in the lives of their students.

There is a healing nature to a judicious approach to student management from which "good vibes" seem to emanate. Constructive, positive, workable, enthusiastic ideas spring from the minds of hall staff focused on student success in college. In many instances, professional staff may only be there to stop the bleeding and are not afforded the opportunity to be around when the wounds begin to heal. However, healing takes time, and only now and then do hall staff experience the extrinsic rewards that are the benefits of judicious management.

Staff must be confident that a democratic community will bring about a successful learning environment in residence hall living. If we do not believe students are able to become a community of responsible citizens, other management approaches will appear more expedient and offer the illusion of better results. The intrinsic rewards of a job well-done, however, have long been the acknowledged legacy of every professional practice.

45

Formulating Rules for Residence Halls

Legal Implications

There are legal limits to the latitude of legislative authority college officials have when structuring rules appropriate to their administrative responsibility. A residence hall floor, for example, may adopt specific rules for themselves as long as they do not violate the rules of the Hall Director and all those in authority above the Hall Director. The rules of the college and state system, in turn, cannot subtend state and federal legislative laws, state and federal case authority, or the United States *Constitution*. In other words, we are all subject to certain "givens"--rules that have been already decided and must be followed by all within their meaning and jurisdiction.

Faced with all the legislative and administrative strata, residence hall staff may feel at a loss trying to locate and assimilate all the pertinent laws and regulations governing their decisions. As a way of bringing this into focus and getting on top of the "givens," three publications should be read and studied carefully.

First, review the rules and regulations published by the campus Director of Housing. These should take into account all housing policies regarding administrative responsibilities and student rights as they relate to residence hall living.

Second, floor advisors should become familiar with the rules of the Hall Director and the regulations applicable to everyone living in the building.

And **third**, know well the college's student handbook and all the rules on campus affecting student activities and programs. Learn the boundaries and the rules you cannot change and make every effort to respect and enforce these rules. If there is disagreement with a rule or decision, discuss it directly with the person responsible for it. It's hard to say this delicately, but violating administrative rules or "the givens" is simply called **insubordination**.

Rules should first be written in broad general terms, inclusive enough to account for all possible student behaviors. The four compelling state interests described previously provide a good outline to follow, and certainly meet the all-inclusive criteria. If, however, these four were the only rules, they would be unconstitutionally vague because of their breadth and, as a result, violate student's procedural due process rights to adequate notice. For instance, a general rule like, "Do not cause damage to the hall," is not specific enough as to what behavior would be injurious to the building. It would not, for example, sufficiently inform students that building lofts in their rooms could be damaging to the interior walls.

An initial broad heading should be followed by examples and preferably a discussion of expected student behavior. The examples need not be exhaustive, but should encompass a number of possibilities in order to bring about student awareness and understanding of the rules. Examples could be from past incidents as well as any problem areas that can be reasonably anticipated.

Rules should be kept to a minimum. The four major headings followed by appropriate examples are easy for students to remember and staff to manage and enforce. This two-pronged approach will address students who argue, "The rules didn't cover that," as well as students who claim, "I didn't know what you meant by the rule." The law does not require college authorities to anticipate in advance and state in writing all of its rules before school begins in the fall. Courts will allow reasonable additions and deletions during the school year. The central question is whether the college can show reasonable cause for the rule change and whether students are given adequate notice before compliance is enforced. Any of the compelling state interests should withstand this test of reasonable cause.

Student Considerations

Of equal importance to the legality of residence hall rules is the message they communicate about how students will be valued. The student handbook and respective living organization rules are, for most students, their first impression of the management style of their residence hall staff. Rules that generate a positive feeling of support help alleviate fears and belligerent attitudes brought on by anticipated encounters many students have with experienced with stereotyped authority figures.

A good beginning would be to develop a hall philosophy statement based on students' human rights and from which all rules and decisions will flow. An example of this is the philosophy statement Corday Goddard and his staff at Wilson Hall on the Oregon State University campus developed for their residence hall. It reads as follows:

> Wilson Hall is a living and learning environment in which all members of the community feel comfortable, involved, and challenged. We are responsible to each other for behavior that exhibits an awareness of respect for human dignity and individual differences. We share the responsibility of maintaining a safe climate that promotes and encourages learning.
>
> As members of this community, students have the right to know the rationale for the rules and decisions affecting them, a right to an equal educational opportunity, and an opportunity to participate in the procedures which ensure these rights. Rights will be denied only when students' individual actions infringe on the welfare and property of others. If a rule is broken, a consequence will be applied that is commensurate and compatible with the infraction. Em-

48

ploying an educational and advising model for solving problems is in keeping with the learning environment.

Our primary goal is to learn to be contributing members of a society which uses a democratic process. It is hoped that students who leave Wilson Hall will possess academic and social skills that will prepare them to function as responsible citizens.

This forceful statement of how students will be valued and respected has become the preamble to the Wilson Hall Constitution as well as being prominently displayed in the main entrance of the building. As with any other philosophy, it has the effect of serving as a constant reminder to students and staff alike of the importance mutual respect has in compatible community living.

Because first impressions are so long remembered, residence hall staff should devote adequate time and planning to carefully shape rules that are clear and concise, and emphasize the behavior desired and the reasons for the rules. Giving reasons for rules and stressing the appropriate behavior has the effect of trusting students to be able to think and act for themselves as well as having the appearance that the rules are not arbitrary or without good reason. For example, instead of, "No loud music allowed in rooms," create a rule which elicits responsible decision making, such as, "Consider the needs and welfare of others when playing music in your room."

Clarify, describe, and teach the behavior acceptable for residence hall living and try to avoid the use of negative statements. For example, "Move carefully in the halls," might replace "No running in the halls." The "do not" rules should be necessary only in case of potentially dangerous situations or in other matters where there is a compelling need for clarity.

Judicious Consequences

When students break rules, residence hall staff usually begin thinking in one of two directions: (1) how shall I confront students with the violation and what would be the most appropriate punishment?; or (2) what more do I need to know about this situation and which advising strategies and campus resources will be most effective in bringing about a reasonable change of behavior?

Both ways of thinking conjure up two very different scenarios, often mutually exclusive. These in turn become the basis for new expectations as consequences are played out. If residence hall staff would direct their thoughts and efforts toward the second approach, utilizing their advising and mentoring expertise as the way to resolve problems, students would not be as likely to perceive consequences as punishing them. They would begin to view the advisor as someone who is working hard to get to the bottom of the situation, providing students an opportunity to recover from their misbehavior as well as giving them time and some help to get themselves back together.

Because a staff member's first disciplinary move sets a definitive stamp on the living group's environment, an underlying philosophy for shaping consequences must be carefully weighed and practiced until, like second nature, it becomes a spontaneous approach to behavioral problems. Having fair and reasonable rules is important, but more often than not, good management is directly related to the way hall personnel handle rule violations as well as student requests for exceptions to the rules.

Rules serve the purpose of providing boundaries and are effective only until they are broken. Once students step outside a rule's boundary, the rule loses its effect. Therefore, when a rule is violated, the burden of maintaining community expecta-

50

tions and changing behavioral attitudes shifts to educational
and workable consequences. Consequences then serve as new
rules for transgressing students. Because of this entanglement
between rules and consequences, **judicious rules necessitate
judicious consequences.**

When there has been a violation of the rules, advisors should
always begin by asking students general questions of inquiry
and concern in an effort to get students to talk about their
perception of what happened. Questions such as, "What seems
to be the matter here?," or "Is there anything I can do to help?,"
or even a descriptive statement like, "Looks like you are having
a bad day," usually encourages students to open up and be
willing to talk about the problem.

Students who talk about themselves in relation to the
situation at hand are beginning to take ownership of the
problem, and as a result, will begin to assume the responsibility
for their actions. By asking relevant questions and listening
carefully, the underlying issues will begin to emerge. As this
process plays itself out and the real problems are uncovered,
responsible decisions become clear, and judicious actions are
much more likely to follow.

On the other hand, if advisors begin by lecturing and
confront nonconforming students with guilt and restatements
of the rules, the message to students is that the advisor owns the
problem and still is assuming the responsibility for students'
actions. Furthermore, students are hearing advisors tell them
that summarily enforcing rules is more important than hearing
students out.

Questions designed to encourage students to talk about their
feelings have the effect of allowing them time to process their
thinking and helping them step back from situations as **they**
begin to take ownership of problems and become responsible for
their own actions. In addition, respecting their due process
rights by showing an interest in hearing their side of the story

51

demonstrates a sense of compassion and justice that tells them that their values and opinions matter.

There are two important aspects of judicious consequences. First, the consequence should be commensurate with the rule violation, and second, compatible with the substantive needs of the student as well as the welfare of the residence hall community. **Commensurate** denotes the consequence is consistent with and flows logically from the student's misbehavior. For example, if underage students are caught with beer in their possession, a commensurate consequence would mean asking them to dispose of it by pouring the beverage out. **Compatible** represents a broader view of the problem, and includes issues ranging from students' need for personal self-worth and academic achievement, to the effect the students' behavior has on college and residence hall environments. Asking students to pour out a beer, for example, would be requested in a manner which was not demeaning, but in respectful manner and sensitive to students feelings in the context of each situation. For instance, "Where do you think the best place would be to pour out the beer?," would be a subtle way of telling someone what is going to happen to the beer and at the same time empowering them with some authority and making them feel they have some say in the matter.

Let's use the two aspects together in another example. A commensurate consequence might logically have a despoiling student scrub graffiti from a wall. But also to be compatible with the student's educational and self-esteem needs, the work could be done when he or she did not have a class and at a time when other students were not around, thus preventing missed classes and ensuring freedom from the ridicule of their peers.

Commensurate or logical consequences are common to many management strategies and provide a good beginning when talking with students about solutions to the problem. But if the logic of the consequence is the only consideration, it can easily degenerate into a contest of matching wits with students as to the wisdom and congruity of the action taken, often escalating into a power struggle and finally to an adversarial relationship.

Take, for example, a group of students talking loudly during announcements during a floor meeting. One action which might be considered commensurate or logical in this situation would be for the advisor to say to the disrupting group, "If you students feel it necessary to talk, then go right on talking. When you finish, the rest of us will be able to continue with the announcements." This method of discipline is called satiation and appears to flow from the disruptive situation. However, not all students would perceive the advisor's statement as only a cue to stop talking, but interpret the approach as demeaning and punishing. Students treated in this way are likely to either talk and talk and keep on talking, or stop talking immediately and never interact positively with the group or the advisor again. Too often students are more responsive to the advisor's conduct and manner with which they handle disruptions, than to the fact their behavior was detrimental to the interests of others.

Because a commensurate consequence is designed only to flow from an infraction, this narrow and one-dimensional focus can obscure other important issues surrounding student problems. Only as students respond to opening questions and comments would an advisor be able to learn whether students are ready or willing to talk about the matter. For example, if students are caught hosing down a hallway with a fire extinguisher, a good beginning would be to inquire about how they believe would be the best way to restore the hallway and replenish the fire extinguisher. If students are not willing to talk about it or ready to remedy the situation, coercing students into a commensurate consequence often side-steps the underlying cause of the misbehavior.

Because of the unpredictable nature of working with students, residence hall staff must also consider carefully the

53

compatible aspect of judicious consequences before deciding what action to take. The compatible nature of judicious consequences embodies an holistic approach and implies a resolution which balances all ramifications and possibilities.

Developing the compatible aspect begins with identifying questions central to the emotional, educational, and self-esteem needs of the student as well as to the mission and ethical practices of residence hall staff. A few examples of professionally responsible questions follow:

1. What needs to be learned here?
2. How can I help the student save face, recover, and get back on track?
3. What is my role as a residence hall advisor in resolving the problem?
4. Do I need more information about the student or the events surrounding the problem?
5. What strategies can we use to keep this student in the hall and in college?
6. How will students perceive what I am trying to do; i.e. help them recover, punish the misbehavior, etc.?
7. How will my actions affect the residence hall community?
8. **And**, in order for the important issues of the problem to unfold and for workable solutions to take form, how can I keep intact the mutual respect needed for a strong student/advisor relationship?

Residence hall staff must examine all the relevant issues of a student's education if they are to develop a judicious style--a professional posture of having authority to decide and act, only after the pivotal questions have been discussed and the real issues have emerged. If asked to retitle *Judicious Leadership*, I would call it something like *When, Where, Why and*

How to Back Off. This is not to be confused with backing down or inaction, but simply an approach to seeing all sides of the question before being responsive to the most important problem. Sometimes, instead of trying to be too inventive or manipulative, hall staff should allow some time for other forces bearing upon the matter to help bring about a resolution or possibly just let what has happened play itself out. Too often needless panic or an exaggeration of the problem exacerbates the situation and an "us against them" mentality pervades.

Residence hall staff must work to instill a certain confidence in students that the residence hall community is in the capable hands of concerned and conscientious professionals. A hammer or a chisel can be very useful tools for meeting some construction needs, but other jobs require the delicate manipulation of tiny Phillips screwdrivers or needle-nosed pliers. The analogy fits the hall advisor who does not try to use a hammer to solve every problem, but carries a tool box filled with strategies and ideas for the purpose of helping students live together successfully. Fair and reasonable rules are without question important but, more often than not, the styling of the approach is decisive in the successful resolution of the problem. Hall personnel with workable ideas are advisors, educators, and administrators with patience and self-assurance.

In determining a judicious consequence for each student, it is important to understand the real nature of the problem as well as account for the **individual differences among students**. For example, suppose two guilty students were asked to clean a vandalized wall and one student replies, "I have the time right after class," and the other belligerently responds, "That's not my job, that's janitor's work.," different judicious consequences for each student might be in order because of their different attitudes. In the case of the first student, the wall would be cleaned willingly, and in all likelihood this would not be perceived as punishment, but rather as an act of restitution from a relieved and conscientious student happy to make amends for the wrongdoing.

As for the other student, another more serious problem has surfaced from the conversation; cleaning a wall suddenly becomes secondary to the defiant attitude now apparent as an underlying problem. This is not the time to get mad at the student or respond with a statement that will be long remembered or act as a roadblock to further communication. This is exactly the time for personal feelings to be kept under control. Advisors must work very hard at being able to look past the immediacy of a belligerent response, and begin to think in terms of a professional commitment to identify and deal with the real source of the student's attitude problem.

Every effort now should focus on resolving the second student's attitude problem. The use of effective communication and problem-solving skills on the part of the advisor as well as the possibility of bringing into play other institutional resources become the important next steps. Judicious consequences directly related to the student's needs are more easily worked out together as the true nature of the difficulty presents itself. Workable resolutions will emerge as the student's belligerence becomes tempered through the advising process as well as with help from other college resources.

Although it may be too late for the second student to clean the wall in question, a subsequent change of attitude could result in the student deciding to rectify his past indiscretion by participating in other cleanup activities or even compensating those who did clean it up. On the other hand, if both students feel they were forced to clean the wall, the first student who did not need to be coerced could resent it as punishment, and the second student's indignant attitude would not only go unattended, but could lead to bitter reprisal and an escalation of further and more serious damage to college property.

One of the problems often expressed when considering

individualizing consequences is the fear that students will fault them as being unfair if others are treated differently. Advisors using punishment as consequences for rule violations are forced to be consistent as students are usually quick to remind hall administrators their punishment was not the same as that which others received for the same offense. On the other hand, by definition, judicious consequences respect individual differences among students and allow more flexibility by styling consequences to meet the emotional, educational, and self-esteem needs of all parties involved. When students perceive consequences as educational, sensible, and know that they are acting on their own volition, students should show little interest in comparing situations.

Group discussions of judicious consequences are an important aspect of student due process rights. Just as students are taught the reasons for the rules, they need to know and discuss the approach residence hall staff will take when working out consequences. For example, during the first few meetings with students, advisors could discuss possible judicious consequences for each of the four compelling state interests and the specific rules protecting the welfare of the hall community.

Under Property Loss or Damage, for instance, questions could be discussed such as; how should we handle a broken light fixture in the lounge caused by student negligence, or what are some ways to resolve the issue of students who are caught taking someone's property? If students participate in developing ideas for judicious consequences at the beginning, students will be aware of what they and their advisor will be discussing if they should have to work through a problem together.

These ideas for consequences should not be summarily applied by the advisor to each infraction of the rules, however, but used as a resource for discussion and development of judicious consequences for each individual situation. The time and effort spent in floor meetings on the commensurate and compatible aspect of judicious consequences will provide the give-and-take needed to establish confidence in the staff's interest and professional ability to reconcile student indiscretions. Staff determination to resolve management problems fairly is directly related to the judicious manner in which consequences are shaped, conveyed, and put into practice.

Residence hall staff should make every effort to avoid voicing or publishing specific consequences before behavioral problems occur. Staff who play their hand prior to the problem often box themselves into a poor decision that, when examined in the light of extenuating circumstances, could have been resolved through use of a more appropriate and instructive approach. Another problem with predetermined consequences is that students often play games with cut-and-dried consequences. For example, knowing that the third infraction for loud music means they will be denied use of their stereo almost invites two disruptions by an irresponsible student. When narrow lines are drawn, students seem to want to stand on them. But staff who draw broad lines that students must walk across, will enjoy better rapport and improved discipline as they confidently allow themselves options and time to work with individual differences.

A judicious style is crucial when working with students who must be removed from the residence hall. It is often pivotal to influencing their attitudes if and when they return. For example, leaving the hall could be meted out as punishment (this will teach you a lesson), or judiciously as an opportunity to get away and cool down a bit (things just didn't work out and we could all use some distance from the problem). The second implies that considerable effort was made to help the student, but a resolution of the problem simply could not be reached. Advisors could keep intact the student/advisor relationship by doing such things as asking students if they need help moving or offering to help them find another place to live. Calling them

58

later to inquire as to how things are going and expressing an interest in the possibility of their return are examples of care and concern inherent in every professional relationship.

Being excluded from a residence hall community is often painful and hall advisors who maintain an open and trustworthy avenue of communication with students who have left do much to alleviate the loneliness and bitterness associated with the separation. Although it requires a little more time and effort, residence hall staff must be sensitive to the self-esteem and academic needs of all students and sincerely care about what happens to them in the future. Helping students in this manner who leave is also a powerful message to those remaining that a judicious style is consistent in helping all students recover and models a leadership attitude and action others may similarly decide to follow.

I have often wondered why some students seem to enjoy finding out what they can get away with on certain residence hall floors but on other floors behave in an entirely different manner. I have come to the conclusion that students find no fun at all trying to disrupt a floor community in which they perceive the floor advisor is making every effort to help everyone live cooperatively and sincerely cares about what happens to all students.

Many argue, however, that judicious consequences are not tough enough and will not deter students from misbehavior. In the short run there may be some validity to these arguments, but if attitudes about the importance of learning and succeeding in college are to be encouraged and exemplified, capable hall advisors will must opt for strategies which will be effective over the long haul.

Residence hall staff who develop a judicious approach to management will eventually earn a level of student trust and respect which in the course of time allows them to transcend the need for establishing consequences for every student misbehavior. If students know that consequences for their misconduct will be judicious in nature, as opposed to punishing, then consequences become educational in nature and not a matter of depriving liberty or property rights.

When students believe they are in the enabling hands of a competent hall advisor, judicious consequences are perceived by students as opportunities designed to help them recover and overcome their behavior problems. As this new level of trust comes about, rules become societal expectations and consequences become professional responses to student behaviors. When this plateau of mutual trust and professional responsibility has been achieved, good educational and ethical practice becomes the model for student management.

Democratic Floor and Hall Meetings

Good residence hall management begins with an advisor's belief that all students should feel they are valued and that they are interested in and capable of responsible social interaction. While it is important to establish appropriate personal and group expectancies necessary for a positive educational atmosphere, it is equally important to communicate to students the fact they are an integral part of successful residence hall living. Often college or hall rules convey the impression that the rules are chiseled in stone, with little or no student involvement.

Ironically, it is not the rules that keep students in college and behaving properly, it is the philosophy and attitude with which college personnel approach rules and consequences that convince students they belong there. In order to create a democratic living organization where students are respected as citizens, students will need to learn something about democratic principles and how they can be put into practice in a residence hall environment.

Soon after students arrive in the hall, there is usually an

orientation meeting in which students are advised of the organization's rules and consequences. This is usually a meeting of all the students living in the hall and normally led by the Hall Director. **Judicious Leadership** would use a part of that session to teach students about the constitutional rights they bring with them to college life, in particular to residence hall living. After some discussion and examples of how those rights can be exercised, the four compelling state interests would be presented as the ways society denies these rights.

A discussion would follow about the importance of the majority's interests and how they form the basis for residence hall rules and decisions. Next could be an introduction to judicious consequences and the rationale behind an educational approach to working things through. Then solicit ideas for possible consequences to some examples of misbehavior as previously recommended. Discuss philosophy and style of management while listening and considering carefully student opinions. Be open and frank about the roles of the advisor and hall director, and that occasionally other resources would be needed to help hall staff work through problems.

This pro-active approach to democratic residence hall living during the first meeting is the single most important statement hall directors and advisors can make. The credibility of the relationship a staff member has established with students before problems arise is directly related to the probability of successfully resolving future indiscretions. For example, in the heat of emotional responses during conflicts with students is not the time to begin establishing a trusting and caring student/advisor relationship. This the time to avoid a counterproductive relationship. A reactive approach to disobedient students is almost never successful and seldom has lasting effect on changing student behavior. A positive, well-thought out pro-active style at the beginning has a healthy effect on establishing positive attitudes and works to circumvent potential student disruptions. A forceful statement of mutual respect from day one will serve as the foundation for a viable and caring student/advisor relationship for the rest of the academic year.

The following are more ideas and a suggested outline staff could use to present this democratic model to their advisees.

1. Briefly review the history of change from college rules based on the concept of "in loco parentis" to today's need to consider student civil rights when developing rules and consequences (see page 30).

2. Talk about how you will approach rules and consequences (see pages 51-67). A possible scenario might be as follows:

I believe it is my professional responsibility not only to recognize and respect your rights as citizens in this residence hall, but to help you live within those rights. Balancing your human rights with our college's need for a livable educational environment will form the basis for our rules and decisions. When it comes to weighing the consequences for rule infractions, we will strive to keep them commensurate with your actions and compatible with your need for personal self-worth and equal educational opportunities (use example on page 52 about student who defaces property or another with which you may be more familiar). I feel it is my responsibility to help you learn about and experience your citizenship rights in this hall and when those rights will be denied, as well as advise you about the demeanor and attitude necessary for all of us to benefit from a good educational experience. If the time comes when your rights must be denied, I will make every effort to be even-

handed as we work through the problem together. Rules and decisions in this hall will
simply be for helping you succeed as a student
living in a residence hall environment.

3. Explain that the 1st, 4th and 14th Amendments are those most often applied to student
rights (see page 22) and how the four compelling
state interests work to deny those rights (see
page 33).

a. Student speech and how it applies to student
expression on campus (see page 77).

b. Students' free exercise of religion and the
college's responsibility not to establish religion
(see page 90).

c. Student press and the distribution or posting
of printed material (see page 86).

d. Student searches and when and how searches
and seizures will be conducted by college authorities (see page 82).

e. The equal protection clause and a student's
right to fair and equal treatment under college
rules and decisions (see page 22).

f. Due process and a student's right to fair and
legal rules, notice, a hearing, and an appeal (see
page 24).

By using examples of how our justice system weighs the
requisites of managing a proper educational living environment
against a person's individual rights, students should be able to
understand and appreciate the fact that their constitutional
rights are not a license to do as they please.

Although this is a lot to present and discuss in one meeting,
part of subsequent floor meetings could be used for further
discussions. As time permits during these meetings, the following approach to Ethics would give the advisor an opportunity to

talk about and reinforce the trust and care necessary to maintaining good, workable student/advisor relationship:

    4. Set forth your ideals about how you view the responsibilities and ethics of residence hall advisors. Some topic ideas to be elaborated upon might be as follows:

    a. Student-centered; recognize the fact that each student brings different educational and personal needs to residence hall living. That your goal is to address individual needs as often as you are able in an effort to help each enjoy college and to successfully complete this academic year (see page 5).

    b. Student/advisor relationship; discuss a student/advisor relationship of mutual respect and care and the importance of continuing this association through good times as well as times when differences may develop.

    c. Positive ethical practices; explain how you feel about your professional responsibilities as a hall staff member and where you plan to direct your energies and priorities (see page 8).

    d. List of "Nevers"; talk a little about what experience has taught you and some things you never want to do again (see page 12).

An open discussion of rules and behavior at the first meeting with students prevents feelings of being excluded from the process and creates a sense of responsibility for community living. By involving the students in a dialogue of reasons for college rules and regulations, residence hall staff are not only teaching citizenship and critical thinking skills, but have brought forth the importance of learning tolerance by modeling a sense of awareness for upholding the individual rights of others. Show students a copy of *Judicious Leadership* and encourage them to read it. If students know it will be the basis for your decisions affecting their property and liberty interests, many may feel motivated to check it out. The return on this investment of time and effort is the students' proprietary interest in their living organization and a feeling of accountability for rules and consequences in which they have participated.

Often administrators believe they are creating a democratic environment when they ask for a consensus from the group or allow students to **vote on an issue.** This does not always accurately reflect our nation's democratic principles and can easily be divisive to a hall's feeling of community in which a close vote on a volatile issue can seriously divide the living organization. For example, a residence hall may vote that abortion literature should not be posted on the bulletin board, or that a single pregnant woman may not run for a student office. Both of these situations involve the rights of students and therefore the rule voted in by the majority would not necessarily make it legal. Students should be helped to understand that voting on the issue is not the way to approach the issue if the matter involves student rights. Our democratic form of government only allows us to vote on those issues which are not protected by the *Constitution.*

Let's use burning of incense as an example. This is an issue common to many campuses and can illustrate how to judiciously resolve a problem of student rights versus governmental responsibility. Students who argue for their right to burn incense as a matter of personal expression or for religious reasons would have a valid rationale and be legally exercising their *First Amendment* rights. However, there may be others who are equally entitled to live in the hall who are distracted from their studies or are allergic to incense and actually suffer serious physical reactions from its use. For a residence hall to vote on whether or not to allow its membership to burn incense in their rooms would result in one of two outcomes; depriving some of their *First Amendment* rights of speech and religion, or, other students of a healthy and educational living environment. Voting on the issue, therefore, would not lead to a satisfactory resolution of either problem.

The issue must be resolved by balancing the needs and interests of both, recognizing our government's authority to regulate students' exercise of their constitutional rights to a reasonable **time, place, and manner**. This should be judiciously handled administratively by the hall's governing body. A small committee could be appointed to look into possible **times** for burning incense, or an appropriate **place** in the building away from student rooms, or a **manner** in which incense could be burned so that the scent could be confined to the person's room. This committee could compile and present a list of reasonable times and/or places and/or manners which balances student rights with the responsibility of the college to provide for the welfare of its students. From this list of recommendations the hall's governing body would then develop rules for the reasonable and responsible use of incense in the residence hall.

There are occasions, however, when voting on residence hall issues would be an appropriate way to decide something and should be encouraged. For example, there should be no problem allowing students to decide, within reason, when quiet hours should be for their floor, which band will play for the hall dance, or whether to have pizza or submarine sandwiches at the Super Bowl party. But on matters affecting student rights and the welfare of the living organization, advisors should teach their students how to develop and employ the judicious administration of reasonable **time, place, and manner.**

The advantage of teaching and administering rules founded on our nation's laws is that **residence hall staff do not personally identify with the rules.** When personal biases are used as the basis for rules and regulations, college authorities are more likely to feel personally responsible and become defensive, thereby causing an escalation of personality conflicts which have no relevance to the student's real problem. A constitutional perspective, however, allows residence hall personnel to remain objective, analogous to a third party whose role it is to shepherd the relationship between the student and society's expectations.

The fruits of this labor are clearly felt when calmly responding to an inquiring or quarrelsome student, "If you are upset by the rules here, you may be surprised by the rules into which you will be graduating." Two hundred plus years of integrated wisdom and legal authority properly presented and discussed can work wonders for residence hall staff seeking to bring about an academic year of mutual regard and respect.

BALANCING RIGHTS
AND RESPONSIBILITIES

Part IV is the synthesis and evaluation of student constitutional rights, good educational practice, and professional ethics counterbalanced with the problems and practical realities of residence hall management. Although some of the subject matter examined may appear to have little to do with good management, the subtle nature of discriminatory practices cuts deep into students' feelings of self-worth and is often the cause for putting students at risk of leaving the residence hall or quitting school altogether.

For instance, how many times would a hall advisor have to repeat or just listen without confronting jokes demeaning a student's ethnic heritage or sexual orientation before students lose confidence in that advisor, or become sullen or despondent, or begin patterns of disruptive behavior? Too often it is an unthinking and insensitive residence hall advisor who spawns and serves as the lifeblood of an uncaring and inhospitable living environment.

Whereas Part II presents a constitutional framework which is well established and has served our nation for two hundred years, Part IV is constantly changing. The dynamics of balancing rights and responsibilities require residence hall staff to stay abreast of new laws and good management practices in an effort to meet society's increasing demands on public colleges and universities.

As we search for ways to create a living environment which models tolerance and provides an equal educational opportunity for all students, keep in mind the scales of justice with a single student on one side looking across at all the other students on the other side. Residence advisors must not only consider and fairly represent the demands of the majority, but also remain conscious and respect the needs and feelings of individual students. This part provides hall personnel a sensible, consistent, and judicious rationale for rules and decisions affecting student behavior.

Enforcing Laws and Regulations

Residence hall staff new to their position should take the time to read carefully the institution's rules and regulations, especially those rules affecting student living organizations. Although knowing all the state and federal laws that govern student life on campus would also be helpful, it is some consolation to know that the unlawful behavior covered by those laws is, for the most part, also covered by the rules of the college and set forth in the catalog, schedule of classes, and the student handbook.

Therefore, knowing and enforcing rules and regulations of the college is generally all the legal authority required for effective residence hall management. However, when a student behavioral matter becomes serious, and state and federal laws are being violated, campus security and law enforcement agencies are available and should be contacted immediately.

One of the most difficult tasks facing residence hall staff is balancing **two** very important aspects of their professional responsibilities. One is that of a **college administrator** charged by the state to enforce its laws and the rules of the institution. The other is the role of an **advisor and confidante** committed to helping each student feel they are part of the residence hall community as well as enjoy and benefit from campus living. The responsibilities of these two aspects sometimes place staff in very tenuous and often difficult positions. A decision one way could have the appearance of weakening one's authority as an institutional administrator, but to approach it another way could put in jeopardy an effective student/advisor relationship.

For example, students violating the drinking laws of the state are committing a criminal act as well as violating college residence hall rules. As college officials, residence hall staff have the responsibility for enforcing the state law and college regulations pertaining to minors drinking on campus. However, as the students' advisor, there is a professional responsibility to help them learn to obey these regulations, to help them deal with problems which contribute to the cause of their drinking, to help them get into bed safely, or to help them obtain professional counseling. Enforcing college rules and regulations as well as maintaining a good student/advisor relationship are both critical to judicious management, and to put either one of these roles in jeopardy, could greatly reduce the integrity and viability of the staff position.

Because of the complex nature of each situation, which is based largely on individual differences among students and the dissimilarities of institutions, there is rarely found a simple or "right" answer as to when a hall advisor should assume the "administrator" or the "advisor" role. We can conclude, therefore, that if neither role by itself can sufficiently resolve every problem presented, then **some consideration of both** must be an inherent part of every advisor's decisions and actions. In some residence halls, however, the action to be taken has been predetermined by hall policy and therefore must be carried out as required, or advisors risk the consequences of being insubordinate.

If the staff members are given authority to exercise some discretion in the matter, they should approach problems by asking themselves **professionally relevant and responsible questions** directly related to the duties of their position: questions which will help them balance the responsibilities of these two important functions. These questions are designed only to begin the process of diagnosing the students' problems, and serve as a springboard for helping advisors define their role in very difficult and, all too often, no-win situations.

To illustrate, let's use the example of a party in process in one of the rooms in which some of the student-guests are under the drinking age. What would be the relevant questions which should be addressed as a way of deciding the best nest steps to take? The following questions are not meant to be an exhaustive list, but an example the types of questions which should come to mind allowing one to back off, not back down, until all the issues have time to surface and be carefully weighed.

"**Administrator role**" questions: Must I report immediately all underage drinking in the hall? Should I visit the room in order to view the extent of the party? Should I remind the host about the rules on room parties? Are there too many in the room? (fire safety) Are they disturbing others? (serious disruption or legitimate educational purpose) Are they damaging college property? (property loss and damage) How can I keep the situation under control?

"**Advisor role**" questions: When should I ask the party-giver about the presence of underage guests, at the doorway in the presence of guests or alone outside with the host? If I ask politely for the party to break up and the guests do not leave willingly, do I deal with the belligerent attitudes now or later? If now, could it be done privately in the hall? If some party-goers were drunk, would later be a better time to talk about excessive drinking? If there is a drinking problem with parties on the floor, would a meeting later on discussing parties in general be a better time to approach the issue?

If students feel they are **living in a democratic environment** where their freedom is always considered and conscientiously balanced with the welfare of the majority, a knock on the door is usually perceived as an inquiry of concern and care about what is happening and to make sure that everyone is all right. On the other hand, if students feel they are living in an autocratic residence hall, where predetermined rules appear rigid and consequences are summarily meted out, then a knock on the door is often perceived as a precursor of a confrontation by an authority figure doing the job of enforcing a "line in the dirt."

Each mindset, by both students and advisors, will generate two almost completely different responses from students who open their door. Unless there is a relationship of mutual respect and care between the student and advisor, the only thing left for advisors is confronting students with lectures about rule violations, what they should have done, and the usual threats of impending punishment. When this reactive approach is taken, an adversarial relationship is quickly established which is usually the cause of a deleterious affect on all other interactions between the parties involved throughout the academic year.

The "administrator role" of **threatening or writing Incident Reports** should be a last resort approach when dealing with disorderly students. Exceptions would be situations considered serious, where authorities require a record of the incident. The "I will report you" approach creates a discomforting uncertainty as to what will happen and is generally perceived as a threatening act which often brings out students' combative nature. To avoid this from happening, every effort should be made to work something out together at the time of the incident. This would not only spare students the mental anguish of something being held over their heads, but allow them to feel they have some immediate control of the situation at hand.

There is also something cleansing about getting past discomforting experiences quickly, for students as well as their advisors, as both are usually relieved and happy when the episode is over and done with. For example, students caught throwing food at each other in the hallway could get out the cleaning equipment right away and clean up the mess. This is likely to be considered by all as a reasonable and responsible act of restitution. "How long do you think it will take us to clean this up?" would be a far better way to approach the students involved than, "I'm writing all of you up for this." If the student/advisor relationship is sound, most of the time students should respond favorably.

Why not join in and **help the students yourself** clean up the food that was thrown? Contrary to how many would interpret this act at first blush, this would not be a sign of a weak authority figure afraid students will not respond to a reasonable request. This would be a powerful message to students from an "advisor/administrator" modeling cooperation, concern for helping others, and caring for and taking pride in the appearance of the residence hall. Advisors cleaning messes made by their students is not a picture of weakness, but of courage, strength, and leadership qualities. Advisors will know they have reached the higher levels of leadership style when they are ready and willing to **model for their students** the behavior they would like to expect in others.

Whenever a situation arises where residence hall staff find themselves "boxed in" by the duality of their responsibilities, the successful resolution of the problem will be directly related to the **pro-active approach** set in motion and reinforced from the first day students entered the building. If students feel that the advisor is really "on their side" in helping them live successfully in a college residence hall, they will understand and accept the fact that advisors must also live with rules that sometimes require them to carry out certain administrative responsibilities they are not necessarily comfortable in doing. When these uncomfortable situations come about, mutual respect for each other's circumstances and good communication become the sustaining forces which keep intact an enabling student/advisor relationship.

Property Loss and Damage

Reasonable rules protecting college and university property are usually well accepted by students. If a problem occurs, it is often because students have not received **adequate notice** that their actions were damaging to the residence hall or the property of others. For example, students who are allowed to put their feet on chairs at home may find nothing wrong with doing it in the lounge. They also may be unaware of the fact that lounge furniture should be left in the lounge for all to enjoy and not carried off to their rooms for their own use.

Identifying and discussing foreseeable problem areas at the beginning of the year will undoubtedly lessen the likelihood of misunderstandings and embarrassment resulting from lack of information. Adequate notice and proper instruction are essential to a fair and reasonable residence hall policy designed to protect property.

Judicious consequences for **damage to public property** should be consistent with and proportionate to the severity of the loss incurred and the students' genuine feelings of remorse. Advisors should communicate with offending students about the logic and importance of making **restitution** for property damaged or stolen. Equipment or materials not returned could result in **loss of privileges** associated with the activity. For example, a volleyball not returned would result in the loss of athletic equipment privileges until returned or paid for. Property taken from **other students** should be returned or paid for, along with a discussion and hopefully an apology for the indiscretion. In some cases, posters displayed outside doors are taken or defaced by unknown others, which can have a dispiriting effect on the whole floor. If the damage is coming from the students in the building, use the group process during a meeting to discuss it, and if it is coming from outside the building, talk about improving hall security and keeping an eye out for trespassers.

The loss or damage of any **student's personal property** is always a matter of concern for residence hall staff. Students should be informed that bringing personal items to college could result in their loss or damage. Students should understand that every effort will be made to help them care for their belongings, but that the residence hall does not have adequate supervisory staff to ensure the safety of all their personal effects. Advisors should inform students soon after they arrive about the problems of property being stolen or even borrowed by others and ways to prevent this from happening.

Rules relating to school and personal property should be perceived by students as a proactive approach involving responsible behavior, with judicious consequences designed for the purpose of changing attitudes and goals. This requires residence hall advisors to teach and promote an attitude of pride in the facilities and respect for the property of others. Group discussions, posters around the building, and occasional complementary and encouraging remarks are a few more ways to help students build and maintain good feelings about their living organization.

A positive educational approach designed to create a protective and caring attitude among students for college and personal property will, in the long run, be far more effective than living in fear of rigid rules and punishing consequences. Those who enter a building for the first time know right away how the people who live there feel about themselves and others around them. Democratic principles can be successful in bringing about a residence hall relatively free from intentional acts of property loss and damage.

Speech and Expression

Speech and expression issues in residence halls can take many forms, one of which is student **dress and appearance**. College residence halls are best served by one broadly written rule communicating the importance of dress and appearance appropriate to a college living environment. The message here is one of respect for the students' ability to decide reasonable appearance in a college setting. Students whom school officials believe are going beyond reasonable bounds could be handled on an individual basis. Students should not be barred from wearing what they choose unless it is **pervasively vulgar**, and until all advising and conference avenues have been exhausted.

Occasionally students or hall staff feel uncomfortable and complain about the offensive **speech or appearance of other students**. In cases where it is not pervasively vulgar, advisors could take that opportunity to help the majority understand that an individual's expression is a self-expression protected by the *First Amendment*. In one situation, for example, a woman was wearing a sweatshirt with the words "Castrate Rapists" printed across the front. During the advisor's discussion with the woman about the statement on her sweatshirt he found that her feelings about this issue were genuine and resolute and that this is exactly what she wanted to express to others. He arranged a meeting with all concerned. After hearing the woman talk about how she felt about rapists and what she was doing about it, the complaining students no longer found the statement objectionable. Advisors should take the time to help their students understand individual expression from a constitutional perspective by providing the forum and leadership for students to communicate and learn from each other to appreciate how other individuals view the world in a residence hall of differing opinions and rich cultural diversity.

Insubordination and open defiance of staff authority not only violates school policy, but is personally infuriating and often difficult to handle without taking it personally. Those in the helping professions, however, learn ways to control emotions and not personalize insolent attitudes, but interpret such behavior as symptoms of other more serious problems. A student who stands up and calls an advisor a "SOB" during a hall meeting, for example, may simply be reacting to a poor grade on an exam or problems that have been developing with a roommate. A visceral reaction of an angry statement in kind by the advisor only makes things worse. Avoid a confrontation by using a more judicious response, such as, "Do we need to talk about this now or can it wait until the meeting is over?" By responding this way, the advisor would not be backing down or condoning the student's language, but exemplifying a professional demeanor and the empathy needed to help a student who may be experiencing a very bad day.

The immediate problem is obviously a defiant attitude, but to modify a student's attitude means getting to the source of the real problem. This can only be accomplished at another time away from the group setting and within the context of a confidential relationship. However, if the whole group becomes defiant, then it must be handled immediately by involving everyone in the group in the same kind of a discussion. If it gets out of hand or other expertise is needed, admit it right away and talk about resolving the problem at another time.

Not every form of student speech is protected by the *First Amendment*; **only ideas are protected**. For example, profane language, indecent gestures, and bigoted statements directed at someone and intended to harass have no protection within the meaning of the *Constitution*. Racial epithets, gender denigration, religious vilification, and cultural disparagement are only some examples of expression which would lead to a serious disruption of the living organization as well as effect the emotional health of the students being harassed. A group discussion setting out examples of sensitive issues would be a good way to help students learn that freedom of speech does not give one license to harass others, and at the same time gives them an opportunity to learn about how others feel.

For example, "Saddam is gay" appeared on a residence hall window at Oregon State University during the Gulf War crisis. The hall director took this opportunity to have a hall meeting which included members of the Gay and Lesbian Association expressing their views about how the statement made them feel. Student attitudes were expressed openly on all sides, which resulted in a growing and learning experience for everyone in the hall. Those offended by the statement learned that opinions and ideas were protected by the *First Amendment* and many students in the hall that evening learned to be more sensitive about homophobic issues.

Because it takes time to process and reflect on new information and simply get beyond the point of defending what was once believed, not all students will become more tolerant after just one meeting. Therefore, time for change must be allowed and continued effort must be made toward helping students understand the value and ways of tolerance. When the sign comes down, it will be because attitudes have changed and not because of a mandate from the hall director. As repugnant and distasteful as these incidents are, they must be met head-on with judicious resolve and leadership in order to bring about a learning experience designed to enable everyone grow and change.

Again we turn to the words of the *Tinker* decision for guidance:

> ...in our system, undifferentiated fear or appre-hension of disturbance is not enough to over-come the right to freedom of expression. Any departure from absolute regimentation may cause trouble. Any word spoken, in class, in the lunchroom or on the campus, that deviates from the views of another person, may start an argu-ment or cause a disturbance. But our *Constitu-tion* says we must take this risk; and our history says that it is this sort of freedom--this kind of openness--that is the basis of our hazardous national strength and of the independence and vigor of Americans who grow up and live in the relatively permissive, often disputatious soci-ety.

Commercial speech in residence halls enjoys only limited protection under the *First Amendment* and is not accorded the purist protection under the law as is noncommercial speech (e.g., statement of political opinion). Students who invite others to their rooms for the purpose of soliciting sale of goods or services can be regulated by reasonable rules. These rules must be neither too broad nor unreasonably restrictive to students' right of free expression.

In the words of the U.S. Supreme Court: "What our decisions require is a 'fit' between the legislature's ends and the means chosen to accomplish those ends...a fit that is not necessarily perfect, but reasonable; that represents not necessarily the single best disposition but one whose scope is "in proportion to the interest served" (*Board of Trustees of State University of New York v. Fox*, 109 S.Ct. 3028, 1989). Legitimate rules covering commercial speech are usually based on the college's interest in maintaining an academic environment, the safety and security of students living there, as well as students' expectancy of privacy.

Student demonstrations often become a part of campus life. Residence hall staff should embrace and support this form of student expression and do everything necessary to help carry out a nondisruptive and safe demonstration. This is a good opportunity to talk with students about their *First Amendment* rights balanced against their responsibility of proper **time, place and manner** based on society's four compelling state interests. For example, students planning a sit-in near the dining hall entrance area to protest the quality of food served need to learn the **manner** of leaving room for others to enter. Those who plan to chant loudly outside the Administration Building about the quality of classroom instruction on campus need to be aware of the best **time** or **place** so as not to disturb classes or students studying.

Residence hall staff could encourage independent thinking and a vigorous exchange of students' ideas by providing bulletin board space in prominent places throughout the hall for various **free speech activities**. Begin with a large one, near the residence hall entrance, as well as one on every floor. It is important for students to feel they have a public forum to speak out on issues of personal interest and public concern. By providing free speech bulletin boards, the college is balancing student rights with the school's need to control the reasonable time, place, and manner of student expression.

In the words of the *Tinker* decision: "....this sort of hazardous freedom...this kind of openness...that is the basis of our national strength...must be balanced with states' interests in providing an educational environment free from serious disruptions." Residence hall staff should not act precipitously or without serious deliberation on issues of student speech and expression. Student, advisor, director, and central office cooperation may be the most judicious course to follow in matters of student expression. Professional hall staff have a duty to help students learn the responsibility that goes with expressing themselves as well as to develop in other students the patience and understanding for those who are.

Search and Seizure

The *Fourth Amendment* of the United State *Constitution* forbids "unreasonable searches and seizures" by government officials and provides that warrants "describing the place to be searched, and the persons or things to be seized" can be issued only "upon probable cause." This amendment is applicable to public college and university residence halls when a state or federal criminal prosecution is based on evidence obtained from college premises and hall staff is involved.

An illegal search will likely bring into play the Exclusionary Rule used by courts to exclude evidence illegally seized. The rule, simply stated, means that evidence acquired in a manner that violates a defendant's constitutional rights is not admissable in a criminal trial. Evidence acquired in a manner that violates the *Fourth Amendment* centers on what is "unreasonable." The reasonableness of the search must be measured carefully against the probable cause requirement and society's legitimate interest in preserving the privacy, integrity, and dignity of its citizens. Although some courts have applied this rule to college and university disciplinary procedures, the trend is away from excluding fruits of an illegal search at suspension and expulsion hearings.

The **"plain view" exception** to the *Fourth Amendment* is an important aspect of reasonable searches. The *Fourth Amendment* only protects one from a search and seizure of property which is concealed, therefore allowing anything in plain view to be seized and legally admitted into evidence. Crucial to this exception is that the staff member, at the time of the viewing, is legally present or acting in accordance with the law. For example, if a residence hall advisor, while walking down a hallway, sees in plain view evidence of drugs through the open door of a student's room, it would not violate the student's constitutional rights for the advisor to enter the room and seize the student's property. By being in the hallway legally and observing the illegal substance through an open doorway, the plain view exception made the seizure legal.

The **four compelling state interests** can be used as the legal rationale to gain entry to students' rooms. For example, housing agreements often stipulate that entrance to rooms will be done for reasons of health and safety (inspect for cleanliness) or property loss or damage (periodic inspections for damage to room or misplaced property). These "housekeeping" type of entries are fairly common, and students should be given adequate notice as to when they will occur.

In **emergency situations** where the health and safety of those in the building is endangered, security should be brought in immediately. In these situations, searches may be conducted on the spot, notwithstanding the fact students are not present or a search warrant was not obtained. A search in the case of a bomb threat or smoke coming from a room would be an example of such an emergency. These housing regulations must be narrowly written and to permit entry and search to be conducted for only the reasons specified in the rules.

In general, **administrative entries must be made in good faith** and directly related to the welfare of residence hall living. They simply cannot be an administrative ploy to circumvent students' *Fourth Amendment* rights, with the underlying purpose being to look for possible criminal activity. It is very important to advise students there will be periodic searches and notify them in advance when and for what reasons the searches will occur. This open and straight-forward approach not only adds to the integrity of good administrative practice in the eyes

83

of the students, but reduces student suspicions that residence hall staff are "sneaking around behind them."

Whenever possible **have students present** when conducting the search. If students are not present, hall staff risk possible accusations of taking something else from a room or desk, or just invading a student's privacy. When students cannot be present, ask another staff member to witness the search and the possible seizure of the student's property. Advisors should leave a message stating their purpose in the room and a receipt for any property that was seized. Although students may give up some of their rights of privacy, they do not give up their **right to notice.** If something is found to be missing in the building, a **random search** of all students' rooms is not advisable and could be a constitutional infringement on their rights. On the other hand, if there was probable cause to believe that a specific student was concealing the missing property, searching that one student's room would be legal.

A common practice in residence hall living is **taking student property** which is being disruptive or not allowed by school rules. Stereos, dangerous weapons, and animals are but a few examples of things occasionally taken and held for the student. Although these items may be properly disallowed, residence hall staff who confiscate property and do not return it within a reasonable period of time, are similarly blameworthy by committing a "tortious taking of another's chattel." Students' personal property should be returned as soon as possible with the exception of illegal items and dangerous weapons. Illegal drugs, firearms, or contraband taken from students should be turned over to campus security or law enforcement authorities immediately. When doing this, ask these officials for a receipt listing the items submitted. Having a receipt could protect you from the embarrassment of accusations that you kept the student's property for yourself.

It is also a good idea to **give receipts to students** when you take their property. Providing a student with a receipt connotes a legality to the action and has the appearance of valuing student's property, as well as providing a record of what and when it was taken. Consider the hypocrisy of summarily taking something from a student as modeling exactly what you are asking your students not to do--that of taking property from other people. By issuing a receipt for those things you take from students or remove from their rooms, what could appear to some as a strong-armed act becomes one of showing respect for the personal property of students. The issue here is one of judicious leadership style and not a question of who has the authority.

Students who **refuse a reasonable request** to relinquish something they are concealing must be handled with caution. Wrestling students to the floor in order to search pockets or back packs may not only result in injury, but be construed later as unreasonable force. Residence hall staff confronted with this situation should not attempt to physically search or seize property, but should rely on the assistance from other staff or deal with the problem at a later time. If students continue to resist and there is danger involved, immediately call campus security or law enforcement personnel.

Although residence hall staff do not have a license to search randomly or invade the privacy of students, they do enjoy the administrative authority to conduct reasonable searches and seizures. By following the college or university policies and guidelines, residence hall staff have all the legal support necessary to manage successfully a safe and secure living environment. Residence hall staff who understand and apply *Fourth Amendment* concepts judiciously should experience few student complaints and feel a greater sense of confidence when dealing with student's expectancy of privacy.

Press

The *First Amendment* freedom of the press clause was set forth to prohibit **prior restraint**. Simply stated, our government does not have the legal authority to mandate in advance what anyone may or may not publish or distribute. However, if a publication injures another person, remedy is through a civil action for libel. In addition, publishing material which advocates the violent overthrow of our government or which is pornographic may result in a criminal prosecution. Civil and criminal actions both may supervene the publication, and wrongdoing will be decided on the merits of each situation.

Therefore, the basic freedom of the press question which faces college and university officials is whether prior restraint or censorship can legally be applied to student publications. As a general rule, the answer is no. In the event of a hall newsletter published by students, for example, the college could not have rules on what the students could not publish.

Unless students in their hall have their own publication, residence hall staff are involved for the most part with questions of hall students as well as outsiders who want to **distribute materials** in the residence halls. These may be in the form of books, pamphlets, or leaflets representing many different kind of ideas and opinions. As with other freedoms, the distribution of these materials may be regulated to a reasonable **time, place and manner**, but cannot go so far as to permit the prior restraint of the message, ideas, or subject matter of the publication.

Time, place, and manner regulations can be formulated by using the **four compelling state interests as guidelines**. For example, nailing or tacking leaflets into walls would damage college property, distributing materials during study time would be in violation of the legitimate educational purpose of the living organization or be a serious disruption, passing out obscene or pervasively vulgar material could affect the mental and emotional health the residence hall students, and bigoted or "fighting words" could lead to a serious disruption.

By using society's rationale for reasonable time, place, and manner, the personal feelings and biases of residence hall staff are not in question, and staff enforcing these rules have the appearance of being personally removed from value judgment decisions. This is especially helpful to remaining self-assured and poised when talking to students who are frustrated and upset when they are restrained from disseminating publications they believe they had a constitutional right to distribute. Although students may not always agree with the decision, most will comply with well-informed and fair staff doing their best to balance society's welfare with the human interests and rights of their students.

There are two very difficult areas residence hall staff must deal with in the distribution of published materials--obscenity and libel. It is clearly within the authority of hall staff to ban obscene and libelous publications. In order to deny the distribution of publications, procedural safeguards must be carefully crafted and constructed to focus as narrowly as possible on the content to be censored.

Obscenity on a college campus is not easily defined and should not be envisaged as "in the eye of the beholder" or as "I know it when I see it." The personal taste and bias of residence hall staff should not be the determining factor; the standard for college residence halls is the same as that of the general community.

The language for these guidelines comes from court cases deciding on the merits of many different fact situations. These guidelines tend to be quite broad in nature, but give us some language we can use when examining the content and explaining our decision to inquiring students.

The following is one example:

> ...A state offense must be limited to works which, taken as a whole, appeal to the prurient interest in sex, which portray sexual conduct in a patently offensive way, and which, taken as a whole, do not have serious literary, artistic, political, or scientific value...(*Miller v. California*, 413 U.S. 15, 24 (1973).

Prurient interest is a phrase used often in court decisions defining obscenity and is generally interpreted as "having or expressing lustful ideas or desires."

A student does not have a right to publish or distribute **libelous materials**. In order for the statement to be libelous, it must be more than just false or misleading. It must also cause at least nominal injury to the person libeled and be attributable to some fault on the part of the person or organization publishing it. Predicting whether distributed material will be libelous is very difficult since injury is only speculative. Moreover, public figures have higher expectations of false and misleading statements and thereby would come under a higher fault standard. Residence hall personnel, for example, would be considered public figures and therefore would come under this higher fault standard. Demeaning statements or outlandish caricatures of their advisors published by students to lampoon authority figures must be "taken with a grain of salt" and just considered as part of the job. Because of its complexity and emotional cost, residence advisors should approach suspected matters of libel with caution. If there is a question about the statement, move it up through administrative channels and possibly to the college's legal advisor.

If students are denied the right to distribute published material, they should be informed about their **procedural due process rights**. To restate briefly, the procedural due process rights of students are notice, a fair hearing, and an appeal.

Applied to student press matters, **adequate notice** means material not permitted (obscene and libelous) for distribution must be stated in a manner that is clear, concise, and reasonably understood by the students. **A fair hearing** means that the student's reasons for not being allowed to distribute the publication must be heard and considered before the decision is conclusive. Finally, the student has the **right to appeal** the decision at the hearing as well as other decisions rendered in the appellate process.

Because residence hall staff must make decisions based on what they believe is obscene or libelous, telling students immediately of their due process rights will usually work to avoid an unnecessary confrontation. A statement such as "I'm sorry you feel that way, but I am going to have to remove your poster because I feel it is libelous to some members of this hall. If you would like to appeal my decision, you should talk to the Hall Director." This avoids an adversarial interaction and has instead the appearance of helping disappointed and sometimes angry students work within the system.

One of the objectives of college living should be to teach the importance of a strong press in a democratic society and, through example, how an educational administration, faculty, and student body can accept and learn from a free and open exchange of ideas. An open and above-board discourse of student and staff opinion should be encouraged and viewed by the administration as an indicator of a healthy educational environment. If college authorities disagree with a student's viewpoints, they can easily disassociate the college from the substantive views expressed by stating or publishing a disclaimer. Students who object to the ideas being distributed by their counterparts should be encouraged to express their views in a similar manner.

Residence hall staff must maintain a delicate balance between students' rights to publish and distribute their opinions with the college's need for responsible student behavior. Unreasonable or heavy-handed censorship of student publications quickly escalates and is often a feature news item in the local press, and on occasion, receives national attention. The fourth estate hangs together very well, vigorously guarding its freedom from prior restraint and thirsting to champion even the smallest of publication injustices. Residence hall staff must make every effort to avoid any unnecessary and unthinking confrontations with student press, or for that matter, any press. Judicious decisions matured by responsible substantive and procedural due process procedures, help everyone learn to appreciate this fundamental right so important to our nation's heritage.

Religion

The *First Amendment* to the *Constitution* provides that "Congress shall make no law respecting an **establishment** of religion, or prohibiting the **free exercise** thereof." When applied to student rights, this double-edged sword forbids a public college or university from establishing religion, and, at the same time requires the college to accommodate the free exercise of its students' religious practices and beliefs. Because residence hall staff are sometimes heavily involved with religious questions of their own as well as those of their students, a good background on church-state issues could be helpful.

A clear, workable, and legal perspective on religious discrimination begins with an understanding of the application of the tripartite test developed by the Supreme Court over many years and brought together in *Lemon v. Kurtzman*, (403 U.S. 602, 1971). **First**, the statute must have a **secular legislative purpose**. Secular purpose usually translates into legitimate educational purpose when applied to most college issues. **Second**, its principal or primary effect must be one that **neither**

advances nor inhibits religion. In other words, college officials must remain neutral and cannot celebrate or advocate a religious point of view, nor can they take a hostile attitude toward religion or impair its worth. **Third**, the statute must not foster an **excessive government entanglement** with religion. There must be a real and ostensible separation between religion and the state. Entanglement matters usually involve control over the use of federal funding and decision-making authority. Campus rules, decisions, and activities must pass all three tests if they are to meet the constitutional criterion of nondiscriminatory residence hall practices.

Although the tripartite test is fundamental to decisions on religious issues, the constitutional concept to keep in mind is the difference between the establishment clause which prevents college personnel from establishing religion, and the free exercise clause which allows students to freely exercise their religious beliefs. For example, individual students who choose to have a Christmas tree as well as other Christmas symbols in their rooms, would be freely exercising their religious belief. But on the other hand, residence hall staff with the same decorations could be making a statement that advances their religious belief, thereby violating the establishment clause. The difference between the two is that rooms of residence hall staff serve a dual purpose, one of which is a state office used daily for the purpose of carrying out the duties of the staff position; whereas students' rooms are used only for personal living and therefore are free to exercise their religious beliefs.

This, of course, begs the question of the residence hall staff and their rights within the meaning of the free exercise clause. Staff do have some free exercise rights, but they must be carefully balanced at all times with their professional responsibilities as a government employee, who by law is not permitted to advance or advocate a religious point of view. It is common to most residence halls that there are many religions and cultural traditions represented. Advisors, therefore, who flaunt their cultural and religious beliefs, put in jeopardy the appearance of respecting and accepting others who do not share the same religious belief. This appearance may seem subtle, but it is essential to the integrity of a viable student/advisor relationship.

Residence hall staff must be discreet about expressing their personal feelings about religion. A small nativity scene or Menorah placed unobtrusively on an advisor's desk would have the appearance of only a personal belief. On the other hand, an advisor's room filled with religious symbols and decorations could be very intimidating and have a coercive effect on students coming into the room for advising or on residence hall business. It is very important, therefore, for advisors to conscientiously balance personal religious convictions with job responsibilities. Students are quick to recognize the difference between an advisor's personal right of expression and one who has the intention of imposing their belief on others.

Residence hall staff who wish to **participate in religious group meetings** should meet somewhere other than in their own hall. In other settings they would not be as likely to reflect the image of a public authority figure and thus not be perceived by others as representing the interests of the college. Hall staff should be respected and approachable as advisors to students of all faith as well as nonbelievers. The balance lies in being very prudent about personal religious beliefs, with that of being cognizant and respectful of the religious convictions of others.

College religious decorations or prayers have the appearance of the institution advancing religion through celebration or worship, and for that reason would seem to violate the establishment clause. However, invocations and benedictions in Congress or at city council meetings as well as Christmas decorations on public property have been held by some courts not to violate the *First Amendment*. These prayers and religious symbols in the public sector have been held constitutional only if they were for a secular legislative purpose. Ceremony, tradition, and its "solemnizing" function are the most common reasons cited for secularizing prayer at public functions as well as "simply a tolerable acknowledgement of beliefs widely held among the people of this country." These legal arguments could be the basis for a college to allow invocations and benedictions at college functions as well the "traditional" Christmas tree as a secular statement reminding students of a religious tradition upon which the coming student holiday is based. As long as it has a secular purpose, it should withstand the establishment test.

In other words, students who ask to decorate the lounge should use symbols depicting the advent of winter vacation as their dominant theme, such as snowflakes, skis, sleds, snow people, families getting together, and a big sign reading "Happy Holiday." A Christmas tree, Menorah, and other religious symbols displayed as part of the decoration would appear as only a reminder of religious traditions celebrated during this time of year and should not have the effect of being there for the purpose of advancing those religions. Just as an aside, an "open forum" could be established and the same area used for these decorations should be made available for other student expressions throughout the school year.

Part of the pain in all aspects of discrimination is the lonely feeling of being "left out." To one whose religious beliefs are not in the majority, the difference between feeling forced to participate in another's celebration and in living in an environment free from systemic coercion can be very subtle. It can appear very lonely to the one who feels outside, and can be all the difference in the world between enjoying and benefiting from college living or being turned off and completely discouraged by the system.

Not unlike other discriminatory practices, religion too can

be the source of frustration and despondency if not handled properly by residence hall staff.

Discriminatory Practices

The *Fourteenth Amendment*, from which all discrimination laws emanate, states in part: "...nor deny to any person within its jurisdiction the **equal protection of the laws.**" From this brief clause federal and state law makers have enacted enabling legislation which protects students from discrimination based on race, national origin, religion, sex, age, handicap, and marital status. In addition, federal and state agencies have promulgated numerous administrative rules which govern discriminatory practices.

This section is not a review of these many laws, but rather a reminder of how a hall advisor's bias and prejudice can have a detrimental effect on students' human rights. Residence hall staff unaware and insensitive to ethnic, cultural, and status issues, and who are unappreciative of the unique differences among college and university students, are more likely to speak and act in ways which result in unequal treatment of students. Only when residence hall staff begin to model and teach the qualities of character which make a diverse nation possible have they met their professional responsibilities as well as the demands of equity appropriate to a culturally diverse society.

Staff who seldom stereotype or label others appear to understand and value the background, culture, and unique differences among their students. These advisors embody qualities which enable them to:

> * Expect the same standards of personal conduct and academic achievement from all students regardless of their ethnic group or cultural tradition.
> * Avoid comparing or ranking groups with re-

94

spect to behavior, attitudes, and accomplish-
ments.
* Avoid the use of descriptive terms, stereotyped
phrases, or participation in humor   that is
derogatory or demeaning to any group of people.
* Promptly admit errors in judgement, sincerely
apologize, and be willing to learn new perspec-
tives.
* Integrate residence hall displays, assignments,
and lectures with various people in different
roles.
* Maintain eye contact, smile, stand near, and
enjoy being an advisor to all students.

One problem facing colleges today is the **sexual harassment** of students by residence hall staff as well as between
students themselves. It is important for staff to understand that
it is the difference in authority, not the intentions of those
involved, that transforms offensive behavior into sexual harassment. Although there is no legal definition of sexual harassment
in education, we must look to federal regulations governing the
workplace for guidelines.

Unwelcome sexual advances, requests for sexual favors, or
other verbal or physical conduct of a sexual nature constitute
sexual harassment when 1) submission of such conduct is made
either implicitly or explicitly a term or condition of an individual's
employment, 2) submission to or rejection of such conduct by an
individual is used as the basis for employment decisions affecting such individual, or 3) such conduct has the purpose or effect
of creating an intimidating, hostile, or offensive working environment (*EEOC Interpretive Guidelines on Discrimination
Because of Sex Under Title VII*, 29 C.F.R. 1604.11, 1984).

Examples of sexual harassment include acts such as sexual
assault, displays of derogatory images of women or men, direct
propositions, subtle pressure for sexual activity, unnecessary

touching, patting, or pinching, verbal harassment or abuse, leering at or ogling of a student's body, and sexual innuendos or jokes about a person's sexual orientation. The effects of sexual harassment or harassment of any nature on students can be overwhelming and have a devastating effect on their success in college. With the current campus atmosphere concerning female student safety, and the heightened awareness of the area of "acquaintance rape," sexual harassment is a major concern on college campuses today.

In and around residence hall living there is always a fair amount of **joking and harassing behavior** among students which not only affects the students who are the target of this humor and harassment, but often can create a hostile and anxious living environment. Whatever form harassment takes or the reason the student is being victimized, it can lead to illness, loss of confidence, decreased concentration, diminished ambition, and depression. In cases of bigoted taunting and teasing, residence hall staff must act immediately and take an active part in bringing about a judicious resolution. If discriminatory acts and statements are not quickly handled, they are likely to get out of hand and result in wounds to students which will never heal completely.

In addition to harassing language and actions, advisors must be conscious of the appearance of their own rooms. Just as with excessive religious symbols and posters that make some students feel uncomfortable and dissuade them from entering, the same is true of expressing other subject matter which might be offensive or in poor taste. For example, students would have a right to a lewd poster in their room, but the same poster in an advisor's room would be a discriminatory practice as well as neglect of their duty as a residence hall advisor. Staff rooms must be a model of tolerance and sensitivity to discriminatory practices, not only as an example for others to follow, but to provide a comfortable and respectful place to carry on hall management activities. If residence hall staff are viewed by all as being resolute in their stand on discrimination and not as a part of the problem--respect, appreciation, and equanimity will soon follow.

Residence hall staff who fully comprehend and believe in the concepts of freedom, justice, and equality are going to encounter fewer problems. Students who feel accepted and understood by those in authority usually have second thoughts about disobeying reasonable rules or taking part in needless disruptions of the living environment. Residence hall staff spend too much time talking and interacting with students to think they can pretend they hold attitudes which they do not. Few study residence hall staff more, or know their biases and weaknesses better than their advisees. Students are keenly aware that the words staff use are only symbols representing what they want others to believe. When words say one thing while gestures and actions another, this is often the antecedent of putting at risk the trust and concern needed for a strong student/advisor relationship. **Judicious Leadership** requires a genuine commitment and conscientious effort to assure all students an equal opportunity to enjoy and benefit from residence hall living.

Health and Safety

One of the important functions of government is the protection of its citizens. This duty is even more important when colleges and universities, through their residence hall staffs, are vested with the duty of protecting students from unreasonable risk arising out of the student/advisor relationship. The importance of student health and safety occasionally surfaces in a lawsuit against the institution, holding those in authority responsible for their negligent acts. While some students may occasionally complain about not being able to skateboard in the hallway or about having to undergo a physical before entering college, most recognize the purpose of these rules and, with appropriate reminders, acquiesce.

In order to be workable and effective, however, rules governing students' health and safety should be:

1. **Well-planned**--Consider what a reasonably prudent residence hall staff member would have foreseen under the same or similar circumstances, periodically inspect for hidden dangers, develop a plan to prevent those foreseeable problems, and follow through with the plan.

2. **Highly Visible**--Use posters, warning signs, verbal reminders, adequate supervision, and other similar measures to insure adequate notice and control over foreseeable problems.

3. **Fully Understood**--Use instructional handouts, verbal explanations, demonstrated student ability, and other communication efforts to teach students the proper health and safety rules, skills, and procedures appropriate for residence hall activities.

4. **Consistently Enforced**--Use proper supervision, be consistent, and "don't even let the Director of Housing skateboard in the building."

As a general rule, there should be a direct relationship between the likelihood of injury and the time and effort devoted to instruction on health and safety precautions. For example, a residence hall's weightlifting apparatus and the technique necessary to use it may require only a posted list of some simple instructions to adequately inform students of its safe use. On the other hand, a hall-sponsored white-water rafting trip would require considerable time and expertise to adequately prepare the participants for a safe outing free from accidents and injuries. There is a direct relationship between the likelihood of student injury and the amount of time and effort spent on proper instructions and adequate supervision designed to prevent those injuries.

Field trips and other **off-campus activities** obviously create a greater need for proper instruction and concern for adequate supervision. Planning for activities off campus should take into account the hazards at the site, risks involved in transporting students, the age and maturity of participating students, as well as anticipating other foreseeable problems related specifically to the location and activities planned.

Liability waivers students sign declaring their knowledge of the risks involved may be in order for some field trips and activities. Inquire with college housing authorities as to their availability and appropriateness when planning off-campus activities, especially when traveling some distance or the activity could be dangerous. Using liability waivers is an excellent way of making clear to those participating any foreseeable dangers as well as providing some protection to the college in case of an injury.

Students who drive their own cars to hall-sponsored activities, especially those carrying other students, should be instructed to follow reasonable safety rules. Advisors should check student drivers for a valid driver's license, adequate insurance coverage, and if possible, evidence of a good driving record.

Residence hall staff have a duty to help students under their care who become **sick or injured**. Those who are competent to administer first aid should do so only up to their level of expertise, and then proceed to obtain other medical assistance. Advisors not trained in first aid should immediately act in accordance with a previously discussed and established plan designed to bring about prompt medical attention. The importance of **following procedures** established by the college or university administration cannot be overemphasized. If there is a lawsuit filed as a result of an injury, the staff member's actions will be judged later on what a reasonably prudent advisor would have done under the same or similar circumstances.

Residence hall advisors should take some time to discuss with students the **importance of following rules** promulgated for the purpose of protecting their health and safety and that without their cooperation, these rules will be very difficult to enforce. Rules requiring that outside doors remain locked after specified hours, the need for their rooms to be locked, and the importance of reporting trespassers are examples of good planning and action designed to prevent theft and harassment as well as physical attacks in the hall. Residence hall staff should ensure **adequate lighting** in and around the building and provide at all times dependable and proper supervision as their part in deterring unwanted entries on the premises.

Residence hall staff cannot afford to compromise on issues relating to students' health and safety. In addition to the tragedy of a student becoming sick or injured, looming in the background is always the threat of a time-consuming and thorny lawsuit as the result of negligent health and safety precautions. If there is a serious injury, begin documenting the circumstances that led up to the injury, what occurred at the scene, and any later information coming to your attention. This information could prove very helpful when an accurate account of the facts could become very important to the attorney representing the college.

Anticipate and plan ways to handle foreseeable dangers, carry through with proper supervision and instructions, and be consistent with enforcement. If the rule or decision is well thought out and supported by sound professional advice, hold firm and do not waver in matters pertaining to student health and safety.

Confidentiality

If there is a vital organ in the body of our *Constitution*, it is the individual's expectation of privacy from governmental action. There is federal legislation, such as the Family Educational Rights and Privacy Act, as well as separate state legislation which often provides specific guidelines concerning the confidentiality of student records and conversations between students and college personnel. Residence hall staff directly impacted by the rules and regulations governing confidentiality must be knowledgeable of and stay current with the applicable federal and state laws. Where these laws do not apply, the principle of professional ethics should be emphasized and prevail.

Although ethics do not represent the letter of the law, this sense of professional responsibility and conscience reflects, in essence, the spirit of our *Constitution*. The following recommendations have their basis in these fundamental principles:

* Consider all conversations with students, colleagues, and parents to be confidential from others, except those who have a demonstrated professional need to know or if the information involves a serious question of health and safety, i.e., suicide, abuse, weapons, etc.

* Take steps to ensure students' academic achievement or behavioral information is not viewed or known by others; i.e., posting of grades, reprimands for rules infractions, etc.

* Avoid comments and visible reactions relating to student behavior in the presence of others. Choose an appropriate time, place, and manner away from others for private conversations to prevent from being overheard. Doing this for

101

both corrective as well as commendatory pur-
poses demonstrates a concern for student self-
esteem needs and avoids many unforeseen problems related to public disclosures.
* Refrain from comparing students with anyone, especially in the presence of other students.
* Discourage students who gossip about the
private life of others.
* Before touching students in any way, give
thought to possible ramifications, i.e., reactions
of students abused as children, sexual over-
tures, right to privacy, tort liability, etc.

Student discipline and academic problems are often directly
related to a residence hall staff member **disclosing information** which, in retrospect, should have been communicated
privately or not at all. For example, telling a student in front of
others at a group meeting that, "Someone whose room is as
filthy as yours should never be allowed to live in a residence
hall," is hardly the time, place, or manner to diagnose or
confront someone about how their personal habits affect residence hall living.

Often statements made by residence hall staff take the form
of a flippant remark or sarcastic comment uttered spontane-
ously in an effort to be clever or entertaining. Many times a
single wanton statement or gesture coming from other students
and reinforced by staff, with even tacit support, can be just as
devastating to the targeted student's feeling of self-worth. Any
disparaging statement about a student made publicly, whether
or not in jest, has the somber affect of diminishing spirit and the
feeling of belonging and, in the long run, often pushing the
student out of residence hall life.

Suicide and other life-threatening disclosures are examples
of confidential communications which must be reported to
qualified and appropriate college authorities. Many student

problems are simply beyond the expertise of residence hall personnel who, while carrying out the responsibilities of their position, become privy to life-threatening information which must be passed on to other professional staff.

In these cases, one-on-one advising should be avoided, and the student should be immediately directed to someone whose duty and training enables them to work with the problem presented. Although a student in some cases may condition a conversation on an advisor's promise not to tell anyone else, in life and death matters or situations that are dangerous to others, the confidential relationship must be abandoned in favor of a professional team approach. This not only will provide better help for the student, but also avoids the possibility of an advisor being a party to a lawsuit for malpractice.

Residence hall staff sometimes hear confessions by students of past **criminal activity**, such as possessing or selling drugs, assault, stealing, extortion, and other similar illegal acts. In the case of only knowing about alleged criminal activity, the staff member is not legally held to disclose the information voluntarily to law enforcement officials. However, staff advisors could be legally implicated as an accessory to the student's subsequent actions if they act or in some way participate in the criminal activity after hearing about the crime. In addition, most states have the authority to subpoena residence hall staff to testify in court about the confidential disclosure of the student's criminal activity. Advisors must be upfront with their advisees and explain to them right away about legal constraints over which they have no control when students begin disclosing this kind of information.

Advising students about abortion, use of contraceptives, conflicts they have with family values, and other similar lifestyle decisions should be done with caution, if at all. Helping students clarify values is a sensitive matter in most situations and precautions must be taken not to become the only professional

103

working with the problem. Advisors should become familiar with and have access to the locations of campus offices or governmental agencies with the expertise and authority best able to respond appropriately to student questions about personal problems. Adverse parental reactions, legal ramifications, and students holding advisors blameworthy are only a few of the possible negative outcomes of imprudent student advising.

Academic advising with regard to degree programs and other college or university requirements should be avoided and every effort should be made to have them make an appointment with an advisor in that particular academic department. Bad or misleading advice from someone not in authority to make academic decisions could result in a student going another term or semester, unneeded costs of living and, in some cases, loss of employment opportunities.

Although there is no federal law that prohibits **tape recording of conversations**, many states have enacted legislation that require all parties to consent to the recording. Ask the student's consent or check state law before taping student conversations.

Students who **demand confidentiality** as a condition for relating a personal problem are asking staff members to compromise their own personal and professional values. If a student says, "I have got to talk with you right now, but you have to promise me you will not tell anyone else," a professional response should be something like, "I cannot promise you confidentiality, but I will promise you that if you choose to tell me your problem, I will do everything I can to help you." Although there may appear to be a fine line between the law and comforting a disillusioned or despondent student, hall advisors must be able to recognize the difference and stay within legal limits and good ethical practice. Emotional involvement is sometimes difficult to avoid, but every effort should be made to maintain a professional relationship. Convince yourself that you are not the only one that can solve a student's personal crisis and solicit the help of the best professionals available.

Whenever possible, residence hall staff should take the time and **walk troubled students to the counseling center** on campus and introduce them to someone there who can be of assistance. Just giving them the location and sending them off seldom gets the job done. Everyone who feels troubled needs a clear-thinking friend nearby who cares enough and knows how to help them take the first steps toward getting the assistance they need. Personal problems of students are frequently volatile and fraught with unforeseen repercussions. Empathetic listening is always helpful and highly recommended, but under very few circumstances would you ever want to "go it alone" with students who have serious personal problems.

Although the confidential relationship between student and advisor is not commonly associated with student management, unprofessional disclosures often precipitate an attitude of mistrust or resentment. On the other hand, advisors who show a respect for students' feelings of self-worth and their right to an expectancy of privacy provide the basis for an open and trusting relationship. Because of this relationship, students will experience a real sense of security and belonging, which in turn forms the foundation of successful residence hall living.

Complaint Procedures

Casting its shadow over every public rule and decision is the *Fourteenth Amendment* right of substantive and procedural due process. Whether or not these rights are stated or written, they are implicit in every public college and university function. How many college catalogs or student handbooks, for example, covering student rights and responsibilities enumerate the students' process for appeal concluding with the United States Supreme Court? Frequently the rationale of an advisor or an

105

administrator is to accord complaint procedures a low profile in the hope that students will be less likely to complain if they remain uninformed. College officials, however, must realize that to encourage student opinion through an accessible and open forum greatly reduces student feelings of frustration, which are often a cause of behavioral problems. For many students, just knowing their opinion will be considered or their grievance heard, gives them a positive feeling about college and assures them that the school has placed a high value on students' rights and interests.

Due process can vary from simply listening to students explain why they had beer in their room to a formal proceeding involving attorneys, witnesses, and a hearings officer adjudicating findings of fact and conclusions of law. Regardless of the level of the hearing or the expertise of the person conducting it, there are three very important procedural due process aspects essential to a hearing's constitutionality. They are as follows.

1. **Notice**--an oral or written notice of the charges. In other words, the student has a right to know what rule was violated.

2. **Evidence**--a summary of the evidence against the student. For example, "Several students witnessed your tearing a poster off another student's door."

3. **Defense**--an opportunity for the student to be heard. This is simply an opportunity for a student to present his or her side of the story.

When residence hall staff are "**hearing students out**" there is no particular model that must be followed. Any procedure which is fundamentally fair, and which allows the lawful authority of the institution to be exercised with discretion, and not arbitrarily or capriciously, is satisfactory. In order to meet the test of "fundamentally fair," however, great emphasis must be placed on interacting with students in a way which does not intimidate or threaten, but in a manner which tends to encourage honest and forthright responses. For example, asking students "What seems to be the problem here?" or even stating the fact that it "Looks like we have a problem here," puts students on notice that something is wrong and, at the same time, does not work to stifle good communication. It also allows students to take charge and decide the tone for conversation to follow. In most cases students know what rule they are violating and often the evidence is quite clear. If not, advisors should take the time to clear it up for students in a non-threatening and helpful sort of way. Hearing their defense and how they view the situation, therefore, becomes the most important aspect of the interaction.

Another problem deals with students who feel more comfortable if they have **someone with them** when talking to an advisor about an incident. A request like this should not only be allowed but encouraged. Students accused of wrongdoing should not be made to feel alone in exercising their due process rights. Other students or staff can be very helpful before, during, and after a hearing, not only for their skill and knowledge, but as friends who can assist them processing and dealing with the overall situation.

In some instances students from another culture have difficulty understanding our rules or trouble speaking English. In cases such as this a staff member should take the time to help those students find someone who is able to represent their interests and interpret for them the college's way of doing things. Sometimes students will ask their advisor to go with them to a hearing across campus that has nothing to do with the residence hall. Take it as a compliment to your abilities and go with them. It is not only a great opportunity to help students, but a real learning experience of how a hearing process feels from the other side.

For **major offenses** and serious problems, hall staff should advise students of their right to a formal hearing on the matter, one that will generally occur at a top administrative level. If there are legal services provided for students on campus, recommend that the student contact a lawyer in that office, or if they would feel better about calling home, the family lawyer may be the best source for providing a name of a good attorney in the area. Regardless of how much advisors feel they know about due process, they should always counsel students that an attorney is their best source of advice in matters of major importance.

Complaint procedures should be specific about who decides what, on what basis it will be determined, and when it will be resolved. For example, if residence hall rules and decisions are discussed first with the floor advisor, and if a satisfactory resolution is not reached, then the appeal process should state the title of the advisor's immediate supervisor and the actionable time frames involved. A similar notice of procedure must be followed through to the institution's chief executive officer. From there the appeal is taken to a board governing the institution. Such a board is the legal entity in every college and university, with final authority for all administrative rules and decisions. If an appeal is denied by the Board, students may appeal to either a federal or state administrative agency or a state or federal trial court, then to an appellate court, and finally, if the justices decide to hear the case, to the United States Supreme Court. To restate it simply, every advisor's decision has the possibility of being appealed all the way up to the United States Supreme Court.

It is important to remember that the complaint process works best if each step is played out properly and none are bypassed. For example, if a student complains about a floor advisor to the Director of Housing, the Director should avoid commenting directly on the problem and diplomatically refer the student to the floor advisor's immediate supervisor. Undermining the authority of subordinates is not only a waste of valuable time, but can dampen the team spirit within an organization as well as diminish student respect for the capabilities and authority of "in-the-trenches" residence hall leaders.

The **decision on any appeal** should be decided within a reasonable time period and communicated as soon as possible directly to the parties involved. If at all possible, resident advisors and hall directors should speak personally with the student. Every effort should be made to be open about the decision and to respond freely and candidly to all questions. If more than one student is interested in an appeal, a conference with all concerned is good administrative practice and has proven to be an effective way to share opinions on sensitive and volatile issues.

Academic and behavioral decisions which effect student liberties and property interests are often placed in the hands of committees. There are problems with this practice. Committees or student courts are not very effective at getting to the source of student problems or enabling them to change their attitudes. The professional student/advisor relationship and judicious consequences are specifically designed for that purpose, and are far better oriented to helping students resolve problems in a confidential and personalized relationship. Students are more likely to open up and talk about their personal feelings to their advisor or hall director than to a committee of their peers.

However, many student life programs have decided to use student committees and courts to mete out appropriate punishments to students who violate the rules. In this case, students who serve on appeals committees must be cautioned about the importance of confidentiality and the problems associated with bias, stereotyping private lifestyles of other students, and peer pressure to gossip or be swayed in making equitable and fair decisions. Because of the importance to the future opportunities of students, student appeals committees should be adequately prepared and properly briefed about the considerable responsibility of deciding on the property and liberty interests of others.

A balance must be maintained between the students' rights to adequate notice, a fair hearing, and appeal, with the college's need for an orderly and efficient operation of its educational living environment. Time taken to implement due process procedures sometimes seems to distract from other educational and administrative responsibilities. However, in the long run, the rewards for respecting and teaching students' due process rights are endless, for the students as well as the college or university. It is my sincere hope that **Judicious Leadership** may be the moving force effusive enough to give an impetus to modeling at least three of our nation's highest moral and cultural values--freedom, justice, and equality.

RESOURCES AND REFERENCES

Legal
I have focused primarily on the synthesis of professional ethics, educational law, and good advising and management practices, and therefore have made a conscious effort to minimize legal language and references. This book is not intended as a legal resource, but rather as a guide to judicious rules and decisions based on legal precedent. Residence hall staff seeking a legal opinion should always consult the legal advisor in their institution or the attorney that will be representing them if litigation from that opinion should occur.

An excellent textbook on legal issues in higher education is *The Law of Higher Education*, 2nd Edition, written by William A. Kaplin and published by Jossey-Bass. It should be on the shelf of every college administrator.

Because laws can change quickly and dramatically, it is essential for college administrators to keep themselves current. The following are publications designed specifically for that purpose:

Synthesis; Law and Policy in Higher Education

is published five times a year by College Administration Publications, Inc., 21 Mt. Vernon Place, P.O. Box 8492, Asheville, NC 28814. (ISSN 1042-0169)

The College Students and the Courts is published quarterly also by College Administration Publications, Inc., at the same address. (ISSN 0145-1472)

The College Administrator and the Courts is published quarterly also by College Administration Publications, Inc., at the same address.

The Association for Student Judicial Affairs publishes a newsletter for their members. For information about this publication write P.O. Box 2237, College Station, Texas 77841.

Case Citations

1. *Meyer v. Nebraska*, 262 U.S. 390 (1923)
2. *Dixon v. Alabama State Board of Education*, 294 F.2nd 150 (5th Cir. 1961)
3. *Tinker v. Des Moines Independent Community School District*, 393 U.S. 503 (1969)
4. *Board of Trustees of State University of New York v. Fox*, 109 S.Ct. 3028, (1989)
5. *Miller v. California*, 413 U.S. 15 (1973)
6. *Murray v. Curlett*, 374 U.S. 203 (1963)
7. *Lemon v. Kurtzman*, 403 U.S. 602 (1971)

Legislation Cited

Federal Educational Rights and Privacy Act [20 U.S.C. Sections 1232g-1232i]

EEOC Interpretive Guidelines on Discrimination Because of Sex Under Title VII, 29 C.F.R. 1604.11 (1984)

ABOUT THE AUTHOR

Forrest Gathercoal is a professor in the College of Education at Oregon State University, Corvallis, and an adjunct professor at Lewis and Clark College in Portland. He has taught law courses for educators for more than twenty years. He has also taught educational psychology, conducted workshops on civil rights and student discipline, served as a consultant to colleges and school districts across the country, and made presentations at many educational conferences. Previously, at the public school level, he served as a classroom teacher, school counselor, coach, and high school vice-principal. While at Oregon State University, he has been director of the career planning and placement office and assistant dean of the School of Education. Gathercoal holds two degrees from the University of Oregon, a bachelor's degree in music and a J.D. from the School of Law. In addition to *Judicious Leadership for Residence Hall Living*, he is author of *Judicious Discipline*, written expressly for elementary and secondary schools, co-author of *Legal Issues for Industrial Educators*, and author of numerous articles on educational discipline and school law.